Penguin Handbooks
Russian Cookery

Nina Petrova was born in Archangel, Russia, of Russian parents. She became stranded in England during the Revolution, when the English ship in which she was travelling to Taganrog stopped in Scotland and her mother became seriously ill. She went to various boarding schools in England, including a convent in Plymouth and the Carlyle School in Chelsea. She finished her education with a year at a French château run by the Grand Duchess of Leichtenburg for Russian refugee children.

Nina Petrova's many and varying jobs include being a secretary, appearing in a film about Pavlova, working in her father's engineering firm, and assisting an artist. After the war she served on a committee for Russian refugees, and arranged buffets at dances in aid of an old peoples' home. She was giving Russian lessons when the aroma of Russian dishes drifted up to the flat of a well-known writer of cookery books who suggested that she should write a book on Russian cookery.

Cooking has always been one of her passions; she is also interested in languages – she speaks fluent Russian and French – and enjoys house-painting ('this is quite a mania') and making hats. Nina Petrova lives in Kensington.

Nina Petrova

Russian Cookery

Penguin Books

Penguin Books Ltd, Harmondsworth, Middlesex, England
Penguin Books Inc., 7110 Ambassador Road,
Baltimore, Maryland 21207, U.S.A.
Penguin Books Australia Ltd, Ringwood, Victoria, Australia

Published in Penguin Books 1968
Reprinted 1970
Copyright © Nina Petrova, 1968

Printed in Great Britain by
Cox & Wyman Ltd
London, Reading and Fakenham
Set in Monotype Joanna

Contents

Introduction

This book was devised firstly because so many of my friends asked me for recipes and secondly because there seemed to be a growing interest in Russian cooking amongst the general public. Russian cuisine, unlike Russian ballet, was until recently little known in this country but it is fast acquiring an international reputation. Our cooking has, of course, been influenced by the French and in fact many French dishes are accepted in Russia as part of the daily menu. English people will be surprised to learn that even English cooking has had an influence on the Russian table. Some puddings and cakes are obviously English in origin and I have left them so. In Southern Russia, many Turkish, Greek and Persian dishes are eaten and I have included some of these too. In fact it is difficult to tell where Russian cooking begins and that of Eastern Europe ends.

Russian cooking is not difficult but it takes a little more time. It is infinitely worth while when you can turn out such famous and delicious dishes as Borshch, Kiev Cutlets, Blini, Shashlik and many others less known but equally tasty. Most of the recipes in this book are simple to follow and can be attempted by the home cook. Russians excel at zakuski (hors d'oeuvres) which should be accompanied by vodka. Soups and casseroles are also first class and there is a good selection to choose from.

If any ingredients are difficult to get from your grocer, Polish delicatessen shops usually stock black bread, cream cheese (curd cheese), salted herrings, etc. Sunflower oil may be obtained from health food shops and large stores. There are many substitutes you can use if the ingredients mentioned are unobtainable or missing from your cupboard. For instance, instead of salted cucumbers which have a short season over here, you may substitute sweet-sour cucumbers in dill either bottled or in cans. These are excellent. Corn-flour or arrowroot can replace potato flour. If there is no sour cream for meat sauces use yoghurt or fresh cream with a little vinegar or lemon juice added. The best results will be obtained if double cream is mixed with an equal quantity of single cream when making sour cream.

Today in Russia, as many young women work outside the home, tinned and frozen foods are used extensively and most people eat their main meal at work. However, good food is still appreciated and the same sort of dishes are eaten as those in this book. I have tried to bring the recipes up to date where necessary to suit modern needs, but without destroying their authenticity. For the hostess with a limited income who wants to be original I thoroughly recommend Russian food, and the busy housewife with a large family should find many dishes to vary the daily menu. I hope you will enjoy the recipes in this book and use it frequently. We have a saying in Russia, 'Po Tzarski', which means fit for a King. I hope after trying my recipes, this is how you will feel.

Zakuski

Zakuski is the Russian word for hors d'œuvres. They can either be tiny open sandwiches served with vodka before a meal or take the form of a cold or hot dish served as a first course. For the open sandwiches use black, brown or grey (a mixture of white and rye flour) bread. There are many different spreads. Pâté, salted herring, smoked cod's roe, anchovies, caviar, smoked sausage and smoked salmon are among the most typical.

Other suggestions for zakuski are to be found elsewhere in the book. Pickled grapes, mushrooms, salted cucumbers and tomatoes (see pp. 177–9) are usually served with vodka. Aubergines stuffed with vegetables (see p. 90) and cucumber or radishes in sour cream (see pp. 95, 97) also make excellent zakuski.

Caviar

The most famous Russian hors d'œuvre is, of course, caviar. It should be served cold, and is usually garnished with lemon. It can also be eaten with blini (see p. 130). Red caviar is excellent on small slices of rye bread.

CAVIAR D'AUBERGINES
(serves 4)

2 aubergines   French dressing (see p. 110)
1 onion   salt
1 green pepper or 3 medium tomatoes

Wash and score the aubergines, brush with oil and bake

them in a dish in a moderate oven (350°F, Mark 4) for about 30 minutes or until tender. Cut them in half and remove all the pulp. Chop. Peel and chop the onion. Chop the pepper or tomatoes, removing the seeds from the pepper, if used. Chop all the ingredients together very finely on a wooden board. Transfer to a bowl and add French dressing and salt to taste.

SALTED HERRING

(serves 4)

1 salted herring
¼ Spanish onion or 1 hard-boiled egg
slices of fresh or salted cucumber

1 tablespoon wine vinegar
1 teaspoon made mustard

DRESSING
2 tablespoons olive oil

If you are unable to buy salted herring fillets from a delicatessen, prepare the whole salted herrings yourself in the following manner. Wash all the utensils thoroughly after use as the smell is very strong.

Soak the fish in cold water, cold milk or strong cold tea for about two hours to prevent it tasting too salty. Put the herring on a double sheet of greaseproof paper. Skin the fish, starting at the neck. Remove the stomach and the head with a sharp knife. Take out all the bones. Wash the fish under the cold tap and drain. Cut in slices about an inch thick and arrange on a plate in the shape of the fish. Put the actual tail and head back in place, spreading out the gills so that the head is fairly flat.

DRESSING: Make the dressing from the oil, vinegar and mustard. Let the dressing soak into the fish before serving as it improves the flavour. It will also prevent the fish from becoming too dry if it is prepared in advance.

Garnish with slices of Spanish onion or hard-boiled egg and fresh or salted cucumber. The yolk of the egg can also be sieved and used as decoration. Serve with potato salad (see p. 100) or Russian salad (see p. 98).

SALTED HERRINGS WITH SOUR CREAM

(serves 4)

2 salted herring fillets	1 sprig dill or parsley or ¼ onion
2–3 tablespoons sour cream	or 2 spring onions

Cut the fish in inch-long pieces and put on an oval dish in the shape of the original fillets. Pour the sour cream between the fillets and garnish with finely chopped dill or parsley, or with onion rings or finely chopped spring onion.

To make a spread chop the above ingredients finely and mix well. Use only 1 tablespoon of sour cream to each large herring fillet. Serve on black bread and butter.

SALTED HERRING PIE

(serves 6–8)

3 or 4 salted herring fillets	1 oz. butter
1½ lb. boiled potatoes	breadcrumbs
½ pt sour cream	

Slice the herrings and potatoes and put them in alternate layers in a greased casserole, ending in a potato layer. Pour in the sour cream. Sprinkle with breadcrumbs and dot with butter. Cook in a moderate oven (350°F, Mark 4) for about half an hour until brown. Serve hot.

SLAV EGGS

To each egg allow:	sprig parsley
knob of butter	breadcrumbs
salt, pepper	

Hard-boil the eggs. Cut them in half through the shells with a very sharp knife. Remove the yolks and sieve them. Mix the yolks with a little softened butter, salt, pepper and chopped parsley. Return the yolks to the whites. Sprinkle with breadcrumbs, dot with butter and grill for a few minutes until brown. Serve hot.

Another version of this recipe can be made by removing both yolks and whites after hard-boiling the eggs. Chop them finely. To four eggs add one ounce softened butter, one tablespoon sour cream and a little chopped parsley or dill. Season and return the mixture to the shells. Finish as above.

KATUSHKI (Meatballs)

(serves 6–8)

1½ lb. raw minced meat (beef, veal, pork or veal and pork)	3 slices stale French bread
1 onion	salt, pepper
	butter for frying

Chop the onion finely and fry it lightly in butter. Remove the crusts and soak the bread in water. Squeeze out the excess liquid. Mix the meat, onion and bread together by hand, adding a little water if the mixture is too dry. Season and form into meatballs. Fry them in butter for about 20 minutes. Serve cold on cocktail sticks with slices of salted cucumber.

This mixture can also be formed into cotletti, coated in breadcrumbs and fried in the same way. These cotletti are softer than those made with egg (see p. 52). They can be sliced and served cold on rye bread.

STUDEN

(serves 8)

½ pig's head	salt
1 pig's trotter	4 peppercorns
1 lb. stewing veal	1 bayleaf
1 onion	2 hard-boiled eggs
2 carrots	a few cooked green peas (optional)

Clean the pig's head and trotter, making sure that there are no hairs left on them. Put all the above ingredients, except the hard-boiled eggs and peas in a large saucepan. Cover with water and simmer with the lid on for about 1½ hours or until the veal is cooked. When it is ready remove it from the saucepan and chop. Leave the pig's head and trotter to simmer for about another hour or until they are very soft. When cooked, lift them out of the stock with the carrots. Strain the stock and skim off any fat. Take a large mould for the studen. Slice the hard-boiled eggs and the cooked carrots and put them with the peas at the bottom of the dish for decoration. Chop all the edible parts of the pig's head and trotter and put them in the dish with the cooked veal on top. Pour in the strained stock and leave to set. When ready, turn out on to a large dish and garnish with watercress. Serve with horseradish cream (see p. 108).

STUFFED TOMATOES

(serves 8)

8 medium tomatoes	2 tablespoons mayonnaise (see p. 109)
2 spring onions	or mayonnaise with sour cream (see
4 hard-boiled eggs	p. 109)
2 sprigs parsley or dill	salt and pepper

Take equal sized tomatoes. Cut off the tops and scoop out

the centre. Salt and pepper the insides. Clean the spring onions and peel the hard-boiled eggs. Chop the onions, eggs and parsley or dill finely and mix them with the mayonnaise. Add salt and pepper, as necessary. Stuff the tomatoes with this mixture and replace the tops. Eat with black bread and butter.

STUFFED BEETROOT

(serves 4)

4 round beetroot (1 ½ lb.)
1 oz. butter
dry breadcrumbs
3 tablespoons sour cream

STUFFING
2 carrots

1 stalk celery
1 small onion
1 sprig parsley
butter or oil for frying
1 oz. rice
salt and pepper

Boil the beetroot (see p. 83) until tender. Remove from the saucepan and allow to cool slightly. Peel off the skin and cut off the tops. Scoop out the centres with a teaspoon.
STUFFING: Prepare the stuffing while the beetroot is cooking. Peel the carrots and onion and scrape the celery. Chop them into very small pieces and stew them, with the parsley, in oil or butter for 15–20 minutes until tender. Meanwhile, boil the rice in salted water. When the rice is ready, strain and mix with the cooked vegetables and any fat left in the pan. Season and stuff the beetroot with this mixture.

Put the beetroot in a buttered fireproof dish, sprinkle with breadcrumbs, dot with butter and bake in a moderate oven (350°F, Mark 4) for a further 15–20 minutes. If ready-cooked beetroot is used in this recipe bake for about five minutes longer. Add the sour cream and serve with meat or game or as a hot zakuska.

Globe Artichokes

Preparation and cooking: Soak the artichokes for an hour in cold salt water to remove dust and insects. Cut off the stalks and the tough outer leaves. Trim the tops of the other leaves to a neat shape with a scissors and remove the choke from the centre. Wash again thoroughly and rub the base with lemon to prevent discoloration during cooking. If they are not to be cooked immediately leave in cold water to which lemon juice has been added.

Cover with boiling salted water in a saucepan and simmer with the lid on for 30–45 minutes, depending on their size and age. When cooked, the leaves will pull out easily. Be careful not to overcook. Drain well and serve with hollandaise sauce (see p. 106).

ARTICHOKE HEARTS WITH HAM AND CHEESE SAUCE

(serves 4)

4 *artichokes*	2 *oz. lean ham*
salt	1 *oz. grated cheddar or gruyère*
1 *oz. butter*	*cheese*

SAUCE
¼ pt *white sauce (see p. 105)*

Prepare artichokes and boil until half cooked. (See above.) Remove the leaves and fry the hearts in butter for a few minutes.

SAUCE: Add the finely chopped lean ham to the white sauce. Put the artichoke hearts into a buttered fireproof dish and cover with the sauce. Sprinkle with the grated cheese and add knobs of butter.

Bake in a fairly hot oven (400°F, Mark 6) for about 15

minutes until brown. Serve as a separate course or a hot zakuska.

LIVER PÂTÉ

(serves 4)

½ lb. chicken or calf's liver
2 oz. green streaky bacon
1 small carrot
1 small onion
1 small stalk celery
½ oz. butter
1 bayleaf
salt, pepper
pinch grated nutmeg

1 dessertspoon Madeira or dry red wine

ASPIC
¼ oz. powdered gelatine
¼ pt meat stock

GARNISH
1 hard-boiled egg
1 salted cucumber

Remove the skin and membrane from the liver. Wash and chop. Cut off the rind and chop the bacon. Clean and chop the vegetables. Melt the butter in the frying-pan and gently stew the liver, bacon and vegetables with the bayleaf. Remove the bacon when it is ready and continue cooking the liver and vegetables until they are tender. Be careful not to over-cook the liver as this will make the pâté dry. Remove the bayleaf and season. Put the bacon, liver and vegetables through a mincer twice. Add the nutmeg and wine. Adjust seasoning, mix thoroughly and form into a loaf shape. Leave to cool and garnish with sliced hard-boiled egg and serve or set in aspic.

ASPIC: Skim the stock to remove all fat. Dissolve the gelatine in a little water and add enough stock to make up ¼ pt of liquid. Leave to cool. When it begins to jell pour it over the pâté, leave to set and garnish with sliced hard-boiled egg.

Serve with Russian salad (see p. 98) or on black bread and butter with slices of salted cucumber.

finely. Mix the fish, bread, onion and egg well by hand, adding a few dry breadcrumbs if the mixture is too wet. Form into a large oval shape and coat in breadcrumbs. Wrap in a napkin or a double piece of muslin. Half fill a large saucepan with water and add the cleaned and chopped carrot and celery, the salt, peppercorns, bayleaf and lemon juice. Bring to the boil and place in it the fish in the napkin. Cover and poach for 25 minutes. When ready, lift out carefully and put on a dish to cool.

Adjust the seasoning in the stock so that it is rather salty. Strain half a pint and dissolve the gelatine in it. Leave it to set.

When the pâté has cooled, transfer it to a clean dish and decorate it with chopped cooked carrot, sliced hard-boiled egg and chopped jelly. Serve with horseradish cream (see p. 108) and beetroot salad (see p. 97).

KATUSHKI (Fish Balls)

(serves 4)

1½ lb. fresh white fish (cod, whiting, hake, haddock or mixture)	1–2 eggs
	salt, pepper
3 slices day-old French bread	breadcrumbs

Remove the skin and bones and put the fish through a mincer. Discard the crusts and soak the bread in water. Squeeze out the excess liquid. Knead the bread, fish and eggs well by hand, to obtain a firm mixture. Salt and pepper to taste. Form into balls about 1½ inches in diameter. Roll in breadcrumbs and steam in a fish-kettle or steamer for about 20 minutes until cooked.

Serve with white wine sauce (p. 107). Katushki can also be eaten cold with Russian salad (p. 98), beetroot salad (p. 97) and horseradish cream (p. 108).

FISH CUTLETS

Follow the recipe for katushki but form the mixture into
rissole shapes instead of balls. Coat in breadcrumbs and fry
for about 20 minutes in oil or fat until golden brown. Serve
with tomato (p. 106) or pickled mushroom sauce (p. 106).

Soups

BEEF BOUILLON OR STOCK

1 lb. beef (topside, silverside
  or chuck steak)
1 lb. beef bones
4 pts water
1 carrot

1 onion
1 stalk celery
1 sprig parsley
salt and pepper

Wash the beef and bones and put them in a saucepan with the cold water. Bring to the boil and remove any scum. Reduce heat, cover and simmer gently. Meanwhile, peel and wash the vegetables. Cut the carrot and onion in half and scorch them gently on a hotplate or in a frying-pan without fat for a few minutes. This gives colour to the soup. Add the vegetables and parsley to the saucepan, bring to the boil, cover and simmer for at least two hours. A little salt and pepper should be added after an hour. When ready, strain and remove any fat.

There are various ways of using the meat from the soup. The most popular is to make it into a pirog (see p. 121), in which case the meat should be removed from the stock after an hour, leaving the bones to simmer for a further hour. The stock will then be rather weak and better used as a basis for other soups than drunk on its own.

For a stronger bouillon the meat should be left to simmer with the bones for about two hours or until the meat is tender. The meat can then be used to make blinchati piroshki (see p. 131) or farshmak (see p. 54). It can also be cut up and put back into the soup or can be eaten as a separate course.

Beef bouillon makes a good stock for frikadelki (p. 24), pelmeni (p. 23) or semolina klyotski (p. 23).

BONE STOCK

2 lb. beef or ham bones	1 leek or onion
4 pts water	2 sprigs parsley
2 carrots	salt and pepper

This is a light stock. Wash the bones and put them in a saucepan with the cold water. Cover and boil for a few minutes. Reduce heat and simmer for 1–2 hours. Skim off any fat formed during cooking. Peel and wash the vegetables and cut them into coarse strips. Add them with the parsley and salt and pepper to the stock and simmer for a further hour. When ready, strain. Use as a basis for other soups.

CHICKEN BOUILLON OR STOCK

1 3–3½ lb. boiling chicken including giblets	1 onion
	2 stalks celery
5–6 pts water	1 sprig parsley
1 carrot	salt and pepper

Wash and truss the chicken and put it in a saucepan with the cold water. Add the giblets, the cleaned and chopped vegetables, and seasoning. Bring to the boil, reduce heat, cover and simmer for 1–1½ hours until the chicken is cooked. Remove any fat formed during cooking. Before serving: strain, adjust seasoning and garnish with parsley.

Chicken bouillon can be served by itself or used as stock for frikadelki (p. 24), pelmeni (p. 23) or klyotski (p. 23).

The boiled chicken can be eaten hot with rice and hollandaise sauce (see p. 106).

SOUP WITH PELMENI

(serves 6)

Use 2½ pts beef, bone or chicken stock (see pp. 21–2)
Pelmeni using ¾ lb. good quality minced beef (see p. 126)
Pastry using ½ lb. flour (see p. 125)

Drop the pelmeni into boiling salted water and simmer for a few minutes to remove the flour. Lift out with a perforated spoon and transfer them to the boiling stock. Simmer for 10–15 minutes, depending on size. Serve the pelmeni in the stock.

KLYOTSKI SOUP (Semolina Dumplings)

(serves 5)

2½ pts beef, bone or chicken stock
  (see pp. 21–2)
¼ lb. semolina
knob of butter

salt, pepper
2 small eggs
sprig of parsley or dill

Bring ¼ pt of the prepared stock to the boil. Add the semolina and a little salt and butter. Simmer, stirring all the time, for about five minutes, until the semolina is cooked. It should be very thick. Remove from the heat, add the beaten eggs and stir well. Cool slightly and form into little balls. Bring the remainder of the stock to the boil, add the dumplings and simmer for 5–7 minutes. Add the salt and pepper to taste. Garnish each plate with a little chopped parsley or dill.

SOUP WITH FRIKADELKI

(serves 6)

3 pts beef, bone or chicken stock (see pp. 21–2)	salt, pepper
½ lb. fresh minced beef or veal	sprig of parsley

Put the meat twice through the mincer so that it is very finely sieved. Add salt and pepper and 1–2 tablespoons of water to form a smooth consistency. Make into small balls of about 1 inch in diameter and drop into the boiling stock. Simmer for 10–15 minutes. Be careful not to let the stock boil too quickly as the meat balls may disintegrate. Serve the frikadelki in the stock. Garnish each plate with a little chopped parsley.

Borshch

Borshch is a soup known all over the world and there are many varieties. It is especially popular in South Russia. The characteristic basis is, of course, beetroot. Served with either pirog or kasha as a side-dish it forms a fairly substantial meal and many Russians dispense with a second course.

Although it is not difficult to make, it takes quite a long time to prepare and is usually made in fairly large quantities to last several days. In fact it tastes better on the second day.

When preparing the borshch it is important to cut all the vegetables finely. The root vegetables should be sliced fairly thinly and cut into strips of 1 to 2 inches by ⅛ inch and the cabbage should be shredded, once the outer leaves and thick veins have been removed. Lemon juice or vinegar is added to the borshch to give it flavour and preserve the colour. A small quantity of raw grated beetroot cooked for a few minutes in a little water will restore colour to the borshch if by any chance it has been cooked too long.

Shchi: This is a cabbage soup which originated in North Russia. The vegetables should be prepared in the same way as for borshch and it can be served with same accompaniments.

UKRAINIAN BORSHCH

(serves 10)

5 pts beef, chicken or bone stock
1½ lb. white Dutch cabbage
2 medium carrots
1 large potato
1 lb. raw beetroot
1 leek
1 onion
½ medium turnip
½ medium parsnip
½ medium swede

1 stalk celery
1 sprig parsley
½ lb. fresh tomatoes or
   2 tablespoons tomato purée
salt
6 peppercorns
1 bayleaf (optional)
juice of ½ lemon
2 teaspoons sugar
½ pt sour cream

Wash the vegetables and peel them, leaving the tomatoes on one side. Chop the onion and parsley finely and cut the other vegetables into fine strips. Put the stock in a large saucepan and add the vegetables, keeping back a small amount of beetroot for colouring. Bring to the boil, cover and simmer for 30 minutes, stirring occasionally. Add the quartered fresh tomatoes or purée, the salt, bayleaf, peppercorns, sugar and lemon juice. Simmer for a further 30 minutes or until the vegetables are soft. Grate the rest of the beetroot and add it to the soup 10 minutes before serving. This will give the borshch a deep red colour. Serve with one dessertspoonful of sour cream per plate.

CLEAR BEETROOT BORSHCH

(serves 5)

2½ pts beef or bone stock or water
½ lb. mixed root vegetables (carrot, turnip, parsnip, etc.)
¾ lb. raw beetroot
1 onion
2 dried mushrooms (optional)
2 peppercorns

1 clove garlic (optional)
1 bayleaf
juice of ½ lemon
1 teaspoon sugar
salt
⅓ pt sour cream

If dried mushrooms are used they should be soaked in a little water for several hours before making the soup. The water they have been soaked in can be added to the stock.

Peel and wash the vegetables and cut them into fine strips (see p. 24). Put all the vegetables, except for the beetroot and dried mushrooms, into a saucepan with the stock or water. Add the peppercorns, garlic and bayleaf. Cover and boil for 10–15 minutes. Add the beetroot and dried mushrooms and simmer for a further 20–30 minutes. Salt to taste. Add sugar and lemon juice. Strain and serve with one tablespoon of sour cream per plate.

COLD BORSHCH

(serves 4)

2 pts water
1 lb. young raw beetroot
salt
1 teaspoon sugar
juice of ½ lemon

2 spring onions
2 hard-boiled eggs
½ fresh cucumber
4 dessertspoons sour cream

Peel and wash the beetroot and cut into fine strips. Put in a saucepan with the cold water and bring to the boil. Reduce heat, cover and simmer for about 30 minutes until the beetroot is cooked. Strain and add salt, sugar and lemon juice. Cool.

Chop the spring onions and hard-boiled eggs finely and peel and slice the cucumber. Add these just before serving together with one dessertspoonful of sour cream per plate. Serve with an ice cube to each plate or chill for 15 minutes before adding the sour cream.

GREEN BORSHCH

(serves 6)

3 pts beef stock	2 stalks celery
1½ lb. spinach	salt and pepper
2 carrots	juice of ½ lemon
½ small turnip	1 teaspoon sugar
1 medium potato	3 hard-boiled eggs
1 onion	6 dessertspoons sour cream

Remove the hard stems from the spinach and wash it thoroughly. Put it in a saucepan with a little salted water. Cover and boil for 15 minutes or until cooked. Sieve and transfer it to the stock together with the water it has cooked in. Peel and wash the rest of the vegetables and cut them into fine strips (see p. 24). Add them to the stock. Bring to the boil and season. Cover and simmer for about 20 minutes. Add the lemon juice and a little sugar and serve with one dessertspoon of sour cream and a little chopped hard-boiled egg to each plate.

MOSCOW BORSHCH

(serves 6)

1½ lb. raw beetroot	½ lb. potatoes
1 onion	1 stalk celery

2 oz. butter

½ lb. tomatoes

1 tablespoon tomato purée

salt and pepper

3 pts water (boiling)

juice of ½ lemon

1 teaspoon sugar

6 dessertspoons sour cream

Peel and wash the vegetables. Chop the onion finely and cut the beetroot, potato and celery into thin strips (see p. 24). Melt the butter in a large saucepan. Add the onion and beetroot, cover and cook slowly for 20 minutes, stirring frequently. Pour in the boiling water and add the potatoes, celery, quartered tomatoes and tomato purée. Salt and pepper to taste and add the lemon juice and sugar. Bring to the boil, cover and simmer for 30–40 minutes until the vegetables are ready. Serve with one dessertspoon of sour cream to each plate.

SHCHI

(serves 8)

4 pts beef or bone stock

1½ lb. white Dutch cabbage

2 medium carrots

1 large potato

1 leek

1 onion

½ medium turnip

½ medium parsnip

½ small swede

1 stalk celery

1 sprig parsley

4 peppercorns

1 bayleaf (optional)

salt

Peel and wash the vegetables and cut them into fine strips (see p. 24). Chop the onion and parsley finely. Add the vegetables to the stock together with the peppercorns and bayleaf. Bring to the boil, cover and simmer for about an hour until the vegetables are cooked. Stir occasionally. Ten minutes before serving add the salt. This soup should be eaten very hot. Serve with one or two tablespoons of hot kasha (see p. 78) in the middle of each plate.

ROSCOLNICK (Kidney Soup with Salted Cucumbers)

(serves 6)

3 pts beef, chicken or bone stock
¾ lb. kidney
1 tablespoon pearl barley (optional)
½ lb. potatoes
1 large onion
1 carrot

1–2 salted cucumbers
1 bayleaf
salt and pepper
¼ pt sour cream
parsley for garnish

Remove the fat and membranes from the kidneys. Put them in a saucepan of cold water and bring to the boil. Remove the kidneys and rinse them under the cold tap. Cut them into small pieces and put them into the prepared stock with the pearl barley. Bring to the boil, cover and simmer for 30 minutes. Meanwhile, peel and wash the vegetables. Chop the onion finely, slice the cucumber and cut the potatoes and carrot into thin strips. Add the vegetables and bayleaf to the stock and simmer for a further 40 minutes. Ten minutes before serving, add salt and pepper to taste. Serve with one tablespoon of sour cream per plate and garnish with chopped parsley.

MUSHROOM SOUP

(serves 5)

½ lb. fresh or 2 oz. dried mushrooms
1 small onion
1 small leek
1 medium potato
1½ oz. butter

2½ pts beef or bone stock or water
1 oz. pearl barley
salt and pepper
2 tablespoons fresh or sour cream

If dried mushrooms are used they should be soaked for a few hours in a little water before cooking the soup. The water they have been soaked in can be added to the stock.

The dried mushrooms should be chopped finely and added to the stock with the potatoes and pearl barley.

Wash and peel the vegetables. Chop the onion and mushrooms finely and cut the leek and potato into strips. Melt the butter in a large saucepan and add the onion and leek. Fry slowly for about 5 minutes, stirring all the time. Do not allow them to brown. If fresh mushrooms are used, add them now. Cook for a further 15 minutes, stirring frequently. Pour in the boiling stock or water and add the potato, and pearl barley and dried mushrooms, if used. Bring to the boil. Season to taste, cover and simmer for a further hour. Before serving, add the cream and stir well.

CREAM OF CARROT SOUP

(serves 5)

2¼ pts beef stock or water	1 egg yolk
1 lb. carrots	4 tablespoons fresh cream
1 lump of sugar	knob of butter
salt and pepper	

Clean the carrots and chop them finely. Add them to the stock or water. Bring to the boil, cover and simmer for 30 minutes or until they are tender. Lift the carrots out of the stock with a perforated spoon and sieve. Return them to the stock and bring it back to the boil. Add the sugar, salt and pepper. Mix the egg yolk with the cream in a cup. Take the soup off the heat and stir in the egg and cream mixture and a knob of butter. Return to the heat for a few minutes, being careful not to allow the soup to boil. This soup may be made with swedes instead of carrots. If so, they should be peeled and chopped finely.

UKHA (Fish Soup)

(serves 4)

4 herrings or 1½ lb. white fish or
    sturgeon
2 pts water
1 teaspoon salt
4 peppercorns

1 bayleaf (optional)
2 medium potatoes
1 small onion or leek
1 sherry glass of dry white wine or
    juice of ½ lemon.

If herrings are used, remove heads and gut. Clean fish and cut into large portions. Put the fish in a saucepan with the cold water, salt, peppercorns and bayleaf. Peel and wash the vegetables. Cut the potatoes into strips and chop the onion or slice the leek. Add the vegetables to the saucepan and bring to the boil. Cover and simmer for 20 minutes. Add more salt to taste and the wine or lemon juice. Simmer for another 10 minutes. Remove fish and serve as separate course. The soup should not be strained; the vegetables are served with it.

Extra potatoes to serve with the fish can be put to cook in the soup about 20 minutes before serving.

LAPSHA (Milk Soup)

(serves 4)

2 pts milk
2 oz. vermicelli
1 teaspoon sugar

pinch of salt
knob of butter

Bring the milk to the boil and add the salt, sugar and vermicelli. Simmer with the lid off for 15 minutes or until cooked, stirring frequently. Before serving add a knob of butter and stir until it melts. Serve with more sugar if you wish.

OKROSHKA (Cold Summer Soup)

(serves 4)

2 pts semi-sweet cider or kvass (see p. 172)	2 hard-boiled eggs
½ fresh cucumber	dill or parsley
2 medium-cold cooked potatoes	salt
1 spring onion	4 tablespoons sour cream

Peel and slice the cucumber. Cut the potatoes into strips and chop the spring onion, hard-boiled eggs and dill or parsley. Salt to taste. Left-over cooked meat can also be chopped into small pieces and added to the okroshka. Mix all the ingredients together and gradually add the cider. Garnish with a little chopped dill or parsley. Chill by putting into the refrigerator for 10 minutes before serving or by adding one ice cube to each plate. Serve with one tablespoon of sour cream per plate.

CHERRY SOUP

(serves 4)

¾ pt water	½ teaspoon cinnamon
1 lb. morello cherries	¼ pt dry red wine
3 oz. sugar	4 tablespoons fresh or sour cream

Stalk the cherries and remove the stones. Put them in a saucepan with the sugar and cold water and bring to the boil. Simmer for about five minutes until they are soft. Sieve and return to the saucepan. Add the wine, cinnamon and sour cream and simmer gently for one minute, stirring all the time. Serve with vanilla rusks (see p. 139).

KHOLODETZ (made with berries)

(serves 6)

1½ lb. fruit (raspberries, strawberries or red currants)	⅓ pt dry red wine
	squeeze of lemon
1 pt water	a little grated lemon rind
6 oz. sugar	¼ pt sour cream

Remove the stems and wash and sieve the berries. Boil the water and sugar for a few minutes to make a syrup. Cool and then add the sieved fruit, the wine, lemon juice and grated lemon rind. Stir well and serve chilled with sour cream and vanilla rusks (see p. 139).

KHOLODETZ (made with chocolate or vanilla)

(serves 6)

3 egg yolks	1 pt single cream
¼ lb. castor sugar	2 sponge fingers per head
½ pt milk	1 meringue or 1 tablespoon
½ vanilla pod	ice-cream per head
½ lb. strawberries or raspberries or ¼ lb. bitter chocolate	

Beat the egg yolks with the sugar in a bowl till white. Put the milk and vanilla in a saucepan and bring to the boil. Remove from the heat and pour over the eggs and sugar, stirring all the time. Transfer the mixture back to the saucepan. If you are making chocolate kholodetz add the broken chocolate now. Cook very slowly over a low heat until the custard thickens. Stir all the time and on no account allow it to boil or it will curdle. Cool the custard and add the cream.

T – R.C. – B

To make vanilla kholodetz, thicken the custard and add both cream and fruit.

Serve with suitably flavoured ice-cream, sponge fingers or one meringue as decoration in the middle of each plate.

Fish

COOKING METHODS

Boiled fish: Do not remove the skin till the fish is cooked. Put the fish in boiling water, cover and simmer for 7–10 minutes to the lb. and 10 minutes over. When cooking white fish add a teaspoon of salt to each pint of water and a little lemon juice or vinegar. This preserves the colour and prevents the fish from breaking. Boiled (white) fish can be served with tomato sauce, horseradish cream, caper sauce, mushroom sauce, hollandaise sauce, mushroom sauce with wine, or pickled mushroom sauce (see pp. 105–9).

Cold boiled fish can be served with horseradish cream, mustard dressing, mayonnaise, or egg and caper dressing (see pp. 108, 109, 110).

Baked fish: Rub fish with salt. Brush with melted butter or oil, dust with breadcrumbs and place in greased baking-dish. Bake at approximately 400°F, Mark 6, 10–12 minutes to the lb., basting frequently.

Fried Fish: Dry fish very thoroughly. Dip in seasoned flour. Fish can be coated in egg and breadcrumbs and can be shallow-fried in oil or butter or deep-fried in oil or fat.

Steamed fish: Allow about 10–15 minutes to the lb. and 10 minutes over. For small pieces of fish use a deep plate over a pan of boiling water. Salt the fish, add knob of butter and cover with another plate. Steam for 10–20 minutes. Use the same sauces as for hot and cold boiled fish.

SOLANKA (1)

(serves 4)

1½ lb. fresh white fish (cod, haddock)
2 small onions
1½ oz. butter
½ lb. tomatoes or 2 tablespoons
  tomato purée
2 salted cucumbers
1 tablespoon capers

1 bayleaf
salt, pepper

GARNISH
parsley or dill
slices of lemon
1 tablespoon olives (optional)

Remove the bones, wash the fish and cut into serving portions. Fry the chopped onions lightly in butter. Add the chopped tomatoes or tomato purée and cook gently for five minutes, stirring all the time. Add the fish, chopped salted cucumbers, capers, bayleaf and salt and pepper. Very little salt is needed as the cucumbers make it slightly salt. Cover with boiling water and simmer for a further 15 minutes. Before serving garnish with chopped parsley or dill, slices of lemon and olives.

SOLANKA (2)

(serves 4)

1½–2 lb. fresh white fish
salt
breadcrumbs
oil for frying
1 onion

2 oz. butter
1 lb. sauerkraut
½ lb. cooking apples
1 tablespoon sugar
1 tablespoon flour

Wash the fish and cut into serving portions. Salt and coat in breadcrumbs. Fry in oil for about 20 minutes until cooked. Meanwhile, peel and chop the onion and fry it lightly in butter in a saucepan. Pour cold water over the sauerkraut, if it is very sour, and squeeze out the excess liquid. Add the sauerkraut, the sugar and the peeled and chopped apples. Cover and cook slowly, stirring from time to time. If the sauerkraut gets too dry add one tablespoon of water. When the fish is cooked, stir the flour into the sauerkraut. Put layers of sauerkraut and layers of fish in a buttered pie-dish, ending with a sauerkraut layer. Sprinkle with dry breadcrumbs and knobs of butter and cook in a moderate oven (350 F, Mark 4) for about half an hour or until brown.

FRIED FISH (with Sour Cream and Cheese)
(serves 4)

1 ½ lb. cod or haddock fillet
salt, pepper
flour
butter or oil for frying
¼ lb. mushrooms
2 hard-boiled eggs

1 oz. grated cheese

SAUCE
1 teaspoon melted butter
½ teaspoon flour
½ pt sour cream

Wash the fish and cut it into slices. Coat in seasoned flour and fry in butter or oil. Clean and chop the mushrooms and fry them separately. When the fish is cooked, put it in a deep dish or casserole and cover with the mushrooms and sliced hard-boiled eggs.
SAUCE: Make a roux from the butter and flour. Heat the sour cream and add it gradually to the roux. Simmer for a few minutes.

Pour the sauce over the fish, sprinkle with grated cheese and put under a hot grill to brown for five minutes.

FISH AND POTATO PIE
(serves 4)

1 ½ lb. cod or haddock fillet
8 large cooked potatoes
⅓ pt milk
2 eggs

salt, pepper
dry breadcrumbs
butter

Remove the skin and cut the fish into fairly small pieces. Grease a pie-dish and fill with alternate layers of sliced cooked potatoes and fish, ending with a layer of potatoes. Mix the eggs with the milk and add salt and pepper. Pour over the fish and potatoes. Sprinkle with breadcrumbs and dot with butter. Bake in a moderate oven (350°F, Mark 4) for about half an hour until brown.

COD PIE (with Sour Cream)

(serves 4)

1½ lb. cod or haddock fillet	⅓ pt sour cream
salt	1 tablespoon butter
1 egg yolk	3 slices day-old French bread

Cook the cod in salted water for 20 minutes. Mix the sour cream with the egg yolk and pour half the mixture into a buttered pie-dish. Remove the crusts and fry the bread lightly in butter. Remove the skin from the cod and fill the dish with alternate layers of bread and fish, ending with a layer of bread. Pour in the rest of the sour cream mixture and brown in a moderate oven (350°F, Mark 4) for about 40 minutes.

ARCHANGEL COD

(serves 4)

1½ lb. cod	3 oz. melted butter
2 lb. potatoes	1 sprig parsley

SAUCE
2 hard-boiled eggs

Boil the potatoes in salted water. They should be ready at the same time as the cod. Clean the cod, cut into serving portions and cook it in salted water (see p. 35). When cooked, strain and remove the skin.

SAUCE: Melt the butter and stir in the chopped hard-boiled eggs and chopped parsley. If the butter is unsalted, add a little salt.

Serve the sauce with the cod and potatoes. This dish is Polish in origin but very popular in North Russia.

DUBLIN BAY PRAWNS (with Cream)

(serves 4)

6 oz. frozen Dublin Bay prawns
salt

SAUCE
1 egg
1 sprig parsley

salt
½ pt cream
pinch of grated nutmeg
1 lemon

Allow the prawns to defreeze and boil for a few minutes to heat through. Beat the egg and chop the parsley. Bring the cream to the boil and remove it from the heat. Add the egg, salt, grated nutmeg and parsley. Return to a low heat for about a minute, stirring all the time. Do not let it boil.

Put the prawns in a dish. Pour the sauce over them and serve with wedges of lemon.

CARP IN WINE

(serves 6)

3 lb. carp
2 sticks celery
4 salted cucumbers
4 sprigs parsley
10 peppercorns
2 bayleaves

pinch of grated nutmeg
1 pt dry white wine
1 pt water
2 tablespoons butter
1 tablespoon flour

Fillet the carp and cut it into serving portions. Put the fish in a large saucepan with the chopped celery, salted cucumbers, parsley, peppercorns, bayleaves and nutmeg. Add the wine and water or salt water from the cucumbers. The fish should just be covered. Cook slowly for about 20 minutes until tender.

Make a roux with the butter and flour. Strain the liquid from the fish and stir it gradually into the roux. Stir until the sauce thickens. Put the fish on a serving-dish and pour the sauce over it.

FRESH SALMON WITH CAPERS

(serves 6)

1½ lb. salmon	1 oz. butter
1 onion	½ pt stock
½ small turnip	1 dessertspoon capers
1 stalk celery	1 sprig parsley
1 bayleaf	pinch of grated nutmeg
4 peppercorns	1 egg yolk
salt	juice of ¼ lemon

SAUCE
1 dessertspoon flour

Clean the vegetables and cut them into small pieces. Put them in a large saucepan or fish-kettle together with the bayleaf, peppercorns and salt. Add water and bring it to the boil. Add the salmon, cover and poach for about 25 minutes. When ready lift out gently and put on a warm dish. Remove the skin and bones and divide into portions. Keep warm while you are making the sauce.

SAUCE: Make a roux from the butter and flour. Strain the stock from the salmon and add it gradually to the roux. Stir until it boils. Add the capers, chopped parsley and nutmeg.

Reduce heat and add the egg yolk, stirring all the time. Heat through but do not allow it to boil. Finally stir in the lemon juice. Serve the sauce with the salmon.

KAMCHATKA CRABS IN WINE
(serves 4)

2 large cooked crabs (about 1 lb. each)
⅓ pt dry white wine
salt, pepper

GARNISH
1 salted cucumber
1 hard-boiled egg
1 sprig parsley

Remove the meat from the shells and cut into pieces. Put into a saucepan with the wine. The liquid should cover the crab meat so add a little water if necessary. Season and cook gently for about 10 minutes with the lid on. When ready, remove from the saucepan with a perforated spoon. Put on to a serving-dish and pour over the liquid. Garnish with sliced salted cucumber, chopped parsley and chopped or sieved hard-boiled egg.

Note: Fresh crabs take from 30–45 minutes to cook, depending on the size.

BREAM IN WINE (with Sultanas)
(serves 4)

1 bream (2–2½ lb.)
¾ pt water
1 carrot
1 stalk celery
1 leek
1 onion
1½ oz. cleaned sultanas
10 peppercorns
1 bayleaf

1 sprig parsley
¼ lemon
¼ pt dry white wine
2 tablespoons vinegar

SAUCE
1 oz. butter
1 tablespoon flour
1 teaspoon sugar

Ask the fishmonger to fillet the fish. Scrape off the scales with a sharp knife.

Peel, wash and chop the vegetables and put them in a fish-kettle or large saucepan with the water. Bring to the boil, cover and simmer for 15–20 minutes. Add 1 oz. of sultanas, the peppercorns, bayleaf, parsley, lemon without pips, wine and vinegar. Put in the fish. It should just be covered by the liquid so add more water, if necessary. Replace the lid and simmer for a further 15–20 minutes. Remove the fish and keep it warm.

SAUCE: Make a roux from the butter and flour. Gradually add half a pint of the strained fish stock, stirring all the time. Add the sugar. A little lemon juice may be necessary if it is not very sharp. Cook the sauce for a few minutes.

Pour the sauce over the fish and decorate with the rest of the sultanas.

TROUT IN WINE

(serves 4)

4 trout (about ½ lb. each)	1 sprig parsley
½ lb. turnip or parsnip	¼ pt dry red wine
1 small onion	2 tablespoons wine vinegar
1 small leek	1 tablespoon rum (optional)
1 stalk celery	
¾ pt water	SAUCE
salt	1 oz. butter
10 peppercorns	1 tablespoon flour
1 bayleaf	

Remove the gills from the trout and gut. Wash thoroughly. The trout can be cooked whole or the heads removed. If the heads are cut off they should be cooked with the fish as they improve the flavour of the stock.

Peel, wash and chop the vegetables and put them with the

water in a large saucepan or fish-kettle. Bring to the boil, cover and simmer for 15–20 minutes. Add the salt, pepper-corns, bayleaf, parsley, wine, wine vinegar and rum if used. Put in the fish head-to-tail. They should just be covered by the liquid so add more water, if necessary. Replace the lid and simmer for a further 10–15 minutes. When they are ready, remove the fish and skin. Keep them warm while making the sauce.

SAUCE: Make a roux from the butter and flour. Gradually add half a pint of the strained fish stock, stirring all the time until it thickens. Simmer for a few minutes.

Pour the sauce over the fish. Garnish with parsley and serve with new potatoes.

TROUT STUFFED WITH KASHA

(serves 4)

	STUFFING
4 trout	1 large onion
salt	3 sprigs parsley
butter	8 tablespoons cooked kasha (see p. 78)
dry breadcrumbs	butter
4 tablespoons sour cream	

Cut the heads off the fish and gut. Wash the fish under a cold tap and salt thoroughly. Coat in breadcrumbs.

STUFFING: Peel and chop the onion fairly finely and fry it slowly in plenty of butter for about five minutes until transparent. Add the kasha and half the chopped parsley and cook very gently for a further five minutes, breaking up the kasha grains until they are quite separate.

Stuff the fish with this mixture. If it is done carefully there will be no need to sew the fish up. Place the fish head-to-tail in a buttered fireproof dish adding just enough butter to prevent them drying out while cooking. Cook in a fairly hot oven (400°F, Mark 6) for 20 minutes. Add the sour cream and the rest of the chopped parsley. Cook for a few minutes longer and serve with the sour cream sauce.

Double quantities of the stuffing can be made and cooked round the fish and served with it.

This dish can also be made with fresh herrings.

STUFFED HADDOCK

(serves 6)

1 whole haddock (about 2½ lb.)	salt
salt	1 onion
dry breadcrumbs	1 oz. butter
butter	

STUFFING
4 oz. rice

Ask the fishmonger to remove the bones from the fish leaving the back skin intact. Wash the fish.

STUFFING: Boil the rice in salted water. Peel and chop the onion and fry it in butter. When the rice is cooked, strain and pour cold water through it. Mix the rice with the onion adding a little melted butter, if necessary, to obtain a smooth mixture.

Stuff the fish with this mixture and sew up with a strong thread. Rub salt well over the fish and coat with breadcrumbs. Dot with butter and put on a greased baking-sheet in a fairly hot oven (400°F, Mark 6) for about half an hour.

STUFFED HERRINGS

(serves 4)

4 medium to large herrings	8 tablespoons stale breadcrumbs
1 onion	1–2 eggs

dry breadcrumbs

oil for frying

salt, pepper

1 lemon

1 sprig parsley

Clean and gut the fish. Dry them and sprinkle with salt. Keep any soft roe for the stuffing.

STUFFING: You may use either white or brown breadcrumbs. Put them in a bowl with the finely chopped roe and onion. Add salt and plenty of pepper and bind the mixture with an egg. It may be necessary to use two if they are small.

Stuff the herring with this mixture. Any left-over stuffing can be fried with the fish and then kept warm until the fish are ready.

Dip the fish in beaten egg and then in dry breadcrumbs and fry in oil or butter for about 20 minutes. Turn once, taking care not to let the stuffing fall out. The heat should not be too high otherwise the fish will burn and not cook through.

Garnish with parsley and wedges of lemon.

UKRAINIAN FRIED FISH

(serves 4)

1 ½ lb. cod or haddock fillet

flour for coating

salt

oil for frying

parsley

SAUCE

2 onions

2 carrots

oil for frying

2 tablespoons tomato purée

¼ pt wine vinegar

2 peppercorns

1 clove

1 bayleaf

Wash the fish and cut it in slices. Coat in seasoned flour and fry in oil until cooked. Cool and put into a serving-dish.

SAUCE: Clean and chop the onions and carrots finely and fry them gently for about 20 minutes until tender. Add the tomato purée, wine vinegar, peppercorns, clove, bayleaf and a little water. Stir and cook through.

Pour the sauce over the fish and allow to stand for a few hours before serving. Garnish with chopped parsley.

JELLIED STURGEON OR HALIBUT

(serves 6–8)

2½ lb. sturgeon or halibut	1 slice of lemon rind
½–¾ lb. hake or pike	1 onion
salt	1 carrot
4 peppercorns	1 calf's foot or gelatine
1 bayleaf	1 hard-boiled egg

Wash the fish and put all the ingredients, except the egg and the gelatine (if you are using this to make the jelly) into a saucepan and cover with boiling water. Cook for about 20 minutes or until tender. Take out the fish and remove the skin and bones. If a calf's foot has been used it should be left to simmer for at least another hour. If gelatine is used mix it in a little cold water and add it to the liquid. (Use ½ oz. gelatine to each pint of liquid.) Strain the liquid and cool. Put the sliced hard-boiled egg and sliced cooked carrot at the bottom of a large dish. Cooked green peas may also be added. Divide the fish into small pieces and put them in the dish. Pour the stock over. Serve when set with Russian salad (see p. 98), horseradish cream (see p. 108) or mustard sauce (see p. 108).

Meat

FILLET STEAK WITH WINE

(serves 4)

2 lb. fillet steak	1 teaspoon flour
1 tablespoon butter	¼ pt red wine
1 tablespoon wine vinegar	salt
1–2 pieces of lump sugar	bouillon or water

Cut the steak into serving portions and grill or cook on a spit for about 5 minutes. Baste meat with a mixture of melted butter and wine vinegar. Burn the sugar in a saucepan and add the flour, wine and enough water or bouillon to make a sauce. Simmer for a few minutes. Put the steak, which should not be completely cooked, into the saucepan, season and stew gently in the sauce for about 20 minutes until tender.

COSSACK STEAKS

(serves 4)

1 lb. rump steak	salt, pepper
2 slices day-old French bread	dry breadcrumbs
1 teaspoon grated onion	oil or butter for frying
1 oz. grated suet (optional)	1–2 tablespoons sour cream
1 egg yolk	1 sprig dill

Chop the meat up finely. Discard the crusts and soak the bread in water. Squeeze out the excess liquid and mix the bread with the meat, onion, suet and egg yolk. Add a little water if necessary. Season and make into four patties. Coat in breadcrumbs and fry on both sides for about 20 minutes. Remove the steaks and keep warm. Stir a little water and the sour cream into the fat to make the gravy. Warm through and pour over the steaks. Garnish with dill. Serve with kasha (see p. 78) and a quarter of salted cucumber per person.

BEEF STROGANOFF

(serves 4)

1½ lb. fillet steak	salt, pepper
1 large onion	1 dessertspoon flour
8 oz. mushrooms	¼ pt stock or water
butter for frying	4 tablespoons cream

Cut the steak into thin strips of about 2 ins. by ¼ in. Peel the onion and chop. Wash the mushrooms and slice them finely. Fry the onion lightly in a little butter for a few minutes. Add the mushrooms and fry for a further 5 minutes, stirring all the time. Add the steak and season. Continue stirring and cook the steak for about 6–10 minutes until it is tender. Mix the flour with ¼ pt stock or water and add it to the beef stroganoff. Bring to the boil, stirring all the time. Cook for a few minutes, then reduce the heat and add the sour cream. Heat through and serve with potatoes or kasha (see p. 78).

BEEF STROGANOFF (with Tomato and Mustard)

(serves 4–6)

2 lb. fillet or rump steak	1 tablespoon tomato purée
salt, pepper	1 teaspoon made mustard
1 large onion	½ pt stock or water
butter for frying	2 tablespoons sour cream
1 dessertspoon flour	

Cut the steak into thin strips of about 2 ins. by $\frac{1}{4}$ in. Peel and chop the onion and fry it lightly in butter. Add the meat, season and cook for about 6–10 minutes until it is tender, stirring all the time. Sprinkle with flour and add the tomato purée, mustard and the stock or water. Bring to the boil, still stirring. Reduce heat and add the sour cream. Simmer for a few minutes and serve with fried potatoes and green salad.

ZRAZA (Meat Roll with Mushroom Sauce)

(serves 6)

6 slices thin top rump steak or topside (about 6 by 4 ins.)	STUFFING
butter for frying	1 onion
salt, pepper	1 2 tablespoons breadcrumbs
$\frac{3}{4}$ pt mushroom sauce (see p. 107)	1 egg yolk

Season the meat and fry it lightly in butter.
STUFFING: Mince or chop the onion finely and mix it with the breadcrumbs, egg yolk and a little water to form a fairly stiff paste.

Put some of the stuffing on to each slice of meat and roll up. Pack the rolls tightly in a greased baking-dish and cover with mushroom sauce. Bake in a moderate oven (350°F, Mark 4) for about half an hour.

CHILAV

Per head:	
	1 oz. butter
rice (according to appetite)	1 egg yolk
salt, pepper	parsley
6 oz.–$\frac{1}{2}$ lb. fillet steak	

The method of cooking the rice is Caucasian and rather

unusual. Soak the required amount of rice overnight in water. Next morning strain the rice in a sieve and pour cold water through. Add a little salt. Put the sieve over a saucepan of boiling water, cover with a lid and allow it to steam slowly until the rice is cooked. Each grain will be separate.

Season the steak, cut it into small cubes, brush with butter and thread on to a skewer. When the rice is ready grill the steak quickly. Serve the rice topped with a large lump of butter, one raw egg yolk and the skewer of steak. Garnish with parsley.

STEAK TARTARE

Per head:

4–6 oz. best fillet or Porterhouse
  steak
1 egg yolk
1 anchovy fillet
1–2 teaspoons French dressing
  (see p. 110)

Cut away any fat and put the steak through a coarse mincer. Add the French dressing. This softens the steak. Mix well and form into a mound with a slight hollow on top. Chill. Before serving garnish with 1 raw egg yolk and 1 anchovy fillet.

HUSSAR'S STEAK

(serves 6–8)

3 lb. joint of roasting beef
½ teaspoon salt
¼ lb. butter or 6 tablespoons oil
1 onion
2 carrots

2 spring onions
3 oz. of grated stale black bread
1 egg
2 oz. melted butter

STUFFING
½ salted herring fillet

Sprinkle salt on the meat. Peel and wash the onion and carrots and slice them. Put them in a saucepan with the butter and fry lightly. Add the meat and fry till it is brown on all sides. Take out the meat and cut into 8 or 9 slices, almost to the end, but leave the slices joined together at the base of the joint.

STUFFING: Chop the herring and spring onions and mix them with the bread, egg and melted butter.

Put the stuffing between the slices and tie the joint with a piece of string. Return the joint to the saucepan adding a little water or stock as necessary. Simmer for about 1½ hours until tender, basting from time to time. Serve with roast potatoes or kasha (see p. 78) and a green vegetable.

RUSSIAN STEW

(serves 4)

1 lb. stewing steak	½ lb. carrots
flour or breadcrumbs	1 thick slice stale black bread
butter or oil for frying	stock or water
2 onions	salt
bayleaf	3 tablespoons sour cream
6 peppercorns	

Trim off the fat and cut the meat into small pieces. Coat in flour or breadcrumbs and fry till brown on all sides. Put one of the peeled and chopped onions, the bayleaf, and the peppercorns on the bottom of a saucepan. Cover with the meat, half the peeled and chopped carrots and the black bread, which should be cut into small cubes. Put the rest of the chopped onion and carrot on top and add enough stock or water to cover. Cook slowly with the lid on for about 1½ hours until the meat is tender. Add salt during the last ten minutes of cooking. Just before serving add the sour cream and heat through.

COTLETTI

(serves 6)

1½ lb. raw minced meat (beef, veal, pork or veal and pork)	salt, pepper
	fat for frying
3 thick slices day-old French bread	dry breadcrumbs
1–2 eggs	1 tablespoon sour cream

Discard the crusts and soak the bread in water. Squeeze out the excess liquid. Add the meat and beaten eggs and mix well by hand. A little water may be necessary if the mixture is too dry. Season and make into cutlet shapes. Coat in dry breadcrumbs and fry for about 20 minutes. To make the gravy, remove the cutlets and keep warm. Add a little water to the fat and stir in the sour cream. Heat through.

Serve with kasha (see p. 78) and a mushroom sauce (p. 107).

ROULETTE

Using the same ingredients as for cotletti, form into a large meat loaf, coat in breadcrumbs and bake in a hot oven (450°F, Mark 8) in a little fat for 1–1¼ hours.

KATUSHKI WITH TOMATOES

(serves 6)

1½ lb. raw minced beef	½ lb. tomatoes or 2 tablespoons tomato purée
3 thick slices day-old French bread	
1–2 eggs	½ teaspoon sugar
salt, pepper	lemon juice
dry breadcrumbs	½ pt water
butter for frying	2–3 tablespoons fresh or sour cream
1 large onion	parsley for garnish

Remove the crusts and soak the bread in water. Squeeze out the excess liquid. Mix the bread, meat and beaten eggs well by hand, adding a little water if necessary. Season, form into meatballs and coat in breadcrumbs. Fry in butter for about 20 minutes until brown. Strain the meatballs and transfer them to a large saucepan. Fry the chopped onion and add to the meatballs together with the peeled and chopped tomatoes or tomato purée, salt, sugar and lemon juice to taste. Pour in enough water to cover the meatballs (about ½ pt). Simmer with the lid on for ¼ of an hour. Before serving, add the cream and warm through. Garnish with parsley.

KATUSHKI WITH PRUNES

(serves 6)

1½ lb. raw minced beef	juice of ½ lemon
3 thick slices day-old French bread	salt
1–2 eggs	2 peppercorns
dry breadcrumbs	1 clove
¾ lb. prunes	bayleaf
sugar	2–3 tablespoons fresh or sour cream

Make meatballs as in the previous recipe. Meanwhile, simmer the prunes in water with a little sugar for about half an hour until soft. Allow one prune to each meatball. Put the prunes and meatballs in a large saucepan and cover with water. Add the salt, peppercorns, clove, lemon juice and bayleaf. Simmer gently with the lid on for ¼ of an hour. The juice is the best part of this dish. It can be thickened with a little flour before serving. Add the fresh or sour cream and warm through.

This recipe comes from the Ukraine.

FARSHMAK

(serves 6)

1½ lb. cooked meat (left-over joint or meat from soup)	¼ small day-old French loaf
	pepper
1 onion	1–2 eggs
1 tablespoon butter	dry breadcrumbs
1 filleted salted herring	4 tablespoons sour cream

Peel and chop the onion and fry it lightly in butter. Mince the meat, salted herring and fried onion. Discard the crusts and soak the bread in water. Squeeze out the excess liquid. Mix well with the meat, herring, onion and eggs. Add pepper. A little water may be necessary to obtain a smooth mixture as cooked meat is inclined to be dry. Coat in breadcrumbs and put into a fireproof dish. Dot with butter and cook in a moderate oven (350°F, Mark 4) for about 30 minutes. Pour the sour cream over the farshmak and serve.

ZRAZA (with Vegetable Stuffing)

(serves 6)

1½ lb. raw minced meat (beef, pork, veal or veal and pork)	1 onion
	2 stalks celery
3 thick slices French bread	1 leek
1–2 eggs	a little swede, turnip or parsnip or a mixture of these
salt, pepper	a little chopped parsley
butter or oil for frying	
dry breadcrumbs	

STUFFING
2 carrots

Prepare the mince as for cotletti (see p. 52). Sprinkle a board with breadcrumbs and roll out the meat.
STUFFING: Clean and chop the vegetables finely and cook

them in butter or oil very slowly for about 20 minutes. Do not allow them to brown.

Spread the stuffing on the meat and roll it up. Put into a greased dish, dot with butter and bake in a hot oven (450°F, Mark 8) for about an hour, basting frequently. Slice and serve hot or cold.

Alternative stuffings are rice and onion, rice and egg or, if it is to be eaten cold, three whole hard-boiled eggs.

GALUPTSI (Stuffed Cabbage Leaves)

(serves 4)

1 large white Dutch cabbage
butter or oil for frying

STUFFING
1 onion
1 lb. raw minced beef
butter or oil for frying
salt, pepper
1 tablespoon rice

SAUCE
½ lb. ripe tomatoes or 2 tablespoons tomato purée
¼–½ pt water or stock
flour
salt
2 tablespoons sour cream

The leaves of the cabbage should be softened before use. The quickest way is to cook the whole cabbage in boiling salted water for about five minutes or until the leaves are soft enough not to break when bent.

STUFFING: Peel and chop the onion finely and fry for a few minutes in oil or butter. Add the meat, season and cook for a further 10–15 minutes until the meat is lightly browned. Meanwhile, boil the rice for about 10 minutes in salted water. Strain and mix with the meat and onion.

Separate the leaves of the cabbage, removing any thick stalks. Place 1–2 tablespoons of the stuffing in the middle of each leaf. Fold in the sides of the leaf and roll up. The leaves can be tied with cotton but it should not be necessary. Fry them on both sides until brown. Remove from the saucepan and pack tightly into a large saucepan or casserole.

SAUCE: Put the peeled and quartered tomatoes and ¼ pt water or stock or the tomato purée and ½ pt of liquid into the frying-pan. Cook gently for a few minutes. Sprinkle in a little flour and add salt to taste. Stir. When the sauce has thickened pour it over the stuffed cabbage leaves. Cover and cook slowly for 30 minutes on top of the oven or for 40 minutes in a casserole in the oven. (Put in at 400°F, Mark 6, turning down to 300°F, Mark 3, after 10 minutes.) Before serving add the sour cream and warm through.

DOLMA (Stuffed Vine Leaves)

(serves 4)

½ lb. young vine leaves	1 lb. raw minced mutton or lamb
mutton stock or water	fillet
½ pt fresh or sour cream or yoghurt	salt, pepper
STUFFING	2 cloves crushed garlic (optional)
1 onion	2–3 tablespoons cooked rice (optional)

Wash the vine leaves in water and cut off the stems. Pour boiling water over the leaves and leave them to soften for about 10 minutes.

STUFFING: Peel and chop the onion finely. Add the meat, garlic and seasoning. Mix in the cooked rice.

Put a teaspoonful of the mixture on to each vine leaf. Fold the leaves over to form small 'parcels' and pack them tightly into a saucepan, adding a little water or mutton stock to prevent them catching. Cover and cook slowly for about three-quarters of an hour. Add the cream or yoghurt and heat through before serving. Some people prefer fresh cream as the vine leaves have a slightly sour taste.

KIDNEYS WITH SOUR CREAM
(serves 4)

1 lb. beef kidney
1 tablespoon flour or dry breadcrumbs
2 oz. butter
1–2 small onions

salt, black pepper
1 bayleaf
¼ pt sour cream
parsley or dill

Skin the kidneys and remove the membranes. Soak in cold water in a saucepan for about two hours. Bring the water to the boil. Remove the kidneys and rinse them in cold water. Cut in slices and coat in flour or breadcrumbs. Do not salt. Fry lightly for a few minutes in a saucepan with the peeled and chopped onion. Add a little water, pepper and a bayleaf. Simmer for about an hour, stirring from time to time. Test with a fork to find out when the kidneys are ready. Add salt to taste and the sour cream. Bring to the boil. Garnish with parsley or dill before serving.

VEAL GOULASH
(serves 3–4)

1 lb. stewing veal
1 onion
½ teaspoon sweet paprika

salt
¼ pt sour cream
oil for frying

Peel the onion and chop fairly small. Fry lightly in the oil. Cut the veal into pieces and add to the onion. Fry together for a few more minutes till the veal is browned slightly. Add a little water and salt. Cover and cook gently for about 1½ hours or until ready. See that the veal does not dry and add more water during cooking if necessary. Towards the end of cooking add the paprika. Stir well.

Before serving, pour in the sour cream, heat through and serve with boiled potatoes and any other vegetables or with kasha (see p. 78).

LAMB WITH WINE SAUCE
(serves 4)

1½ lb. leg of lamb (boned) or 4 lamb chops	1 dessertspoon flour
1 carrot	½ pt stock
1 onion	1 lump sugar
salt	juice of ½ lemon
5 peppercorns	¼ pt dry red wine
1 bayleaf	1 egg yolk

SAUCE
½ oz. butter

Take 4 lamb chops or thick slices from a leg of lamb and put them in a saucepan. Cover with water and bring to the boil. Strain the liquid and return it to the saucepan. Add the peeled onion and carrot. Cover and simmer for about 40 minutes until tender. Add the salt, peppercorns and the bayleaf and simmer for a further few minutes.

SAUCE: Make a roux from the butter and flour in a separate saucepan. Gradually add about half a pint of stock from the meat, or stock and water, to make a smooth sauce. Add the sugar, lemon juice and wine. Bring to the boil. Remove from the heat and stir in the egg yolk. Heat through but do not boil.

Put the lamb on a serving-dish and pour over the sauce. Serve with kasha (see p. 78).

SHASHLIK
(serves 4)

1½ lb. lamb or mutton off the leg	1 clove garlic (optional)
1 large onion	wine vinegar
1 spring onion (optional)	salt, pepper
1 lemon (optional)	

Cut the meat into small pieces suitable for putting on skewers. Put in a cool place with half the peeled and finely chopped onion and garlic if used. Cover with a mixture of wine vinegar and water in equal parts. Marinate for 2–3 hours. Drain the meat, season and thread on skewers interspersed with the remainder of onion cut into rings. Grill or cook on a spit for 10–15 minutes. If you grill the shashlik they should be turned frequently. Serve on the skewer in the middle of a bed of hot rice. If desired pour over a little melted butter before serving.

The shashlik can be garnished with slices of lemon or chopped spring onion if you wish.

This is a Caucasian dish.

UKRAINIAN LAMB CHOPS
(serves 4)

4 lamb chops	2 teaspoons sugar
6 oz. prunes	2 teaspoons vinegar
1 onion	1 clove
1 teaspoon tomato purée	pinch of cinnamon
stock or water	1 teaspoon flour
salt, pepper	

Dried prunes should be soaked in water overnight. Californian prunes, however, can be cooked immediately.

Fry the chops in a little lamb fat or grill for a few minutes until brown. Put them in a suitable saucepan and add the peeled and chopped onion and the tomato purée. Cover with stock or water and simmer gently with the lid on for about ten minutes. Add the remaining ingredients except the flour. Simmer for a further 30 minutes or until both the chops and prunes are tender. Remove the chops and prunes and keep them warm. Thicken the liquid in the saucepan with a teaspoon of flour mixed with a little water. Simmer for a few minutes, stirring all the time. Serve with the chops and prunes.

UZBECK PLOV (Lamb and Rice)
(serves 4)

1 lb. lamb	1½ pts water
oil or butter for frying	salt
1 large onion	4 peppercorns
1 lb. carrots	chopped parsley
12 oz. rice	

Heat the butter or oil in a fairly large saucepan. Add the peeled and chopped onion and fry till golden brown. Cut the meat into small pieces and add to the onion and brown lightly. Add the peeled and finely chopped carrots and stew for about 30 minutes until tender, stirring frequently. Wash the rice several times in cold water. Add to the meat together with 1½ pts water, the salt and peppercorns. Cover and cook slowly for about 15 minutes until the rice has absorbed all the water. Garnish with chopped parsley.

TURKMENIAN PILAF
(serves 4)

1½ lb. leg of lamb (or chicken or veal)	1 pt stock or water
¼ lb. prunes	1 onion
1 tablespoon sultanas	2 oz. butter
¼ lemon	salt
8 oz. rice	4 peppercorns

Cover the dried fruit with boiling water. Add the lemon and leave to stand while the lamb is cooking. Wash the rice several times in cold water, cover with boiling water and leave to stand. Salt the lamb and cut it into small pieces. Peel and chop the onion and fry it lightly in butter. Add the lamb and brown lightly. Cover with stock or water, add the peppercorns and simmer with the lid on for 25 minutes. Strain the rice and pour cold water through. Add to the meat together with the strained prunes and sultanas. Pour in enough stock or water to cover and adjust seasoning. Cook slowly with the lid on until the rice has absorbed all the stock. It should take about 20 minutes in a saucepan or 30 minutes in a casserole (350°F, Mark 4).

BRAISED SHOULDER OF VEAL
(serves 4–5)

2 lb. shoulder of veal	oil for cooking
salt	1 onion
1 clove garlic	¼ pt dry white wine
sprig rosemary	¼ pt water

Ask the butcher to bone half a shoulder of veal. Salt and rub with garlic. Sprinkle with a little rosemary. Roll and tie with string. Peel the onion but do not slice. Put the veal and onion in a saucepan with the oil and brown meat all over. After half an hour pour off the excess fat and add the wine and water. Cover and simmer for a further hour or until ready, basting frequently. This may be eaten hot or cold. If it is to be served cold, put the meat into a serving-dish, pour the gravy over and leave to set into a jelly.

SOLANKA (Sauerkraut and Meat)
(serves 4–5)

1 onion	salt
1–1½ lb. sauerkraut	½ teaspoon sugar (optional)
2 oz. butter	1 lb. cooked ham or cooked pork
2 peppercorns	¼ lb. garlic sausage
1 bayleaf	

If the sauerkraut is very sour run cold water through and squeeze out the excess liquid. Chop the onion and fry it lightly in butter. Add the sauerkraut, cover and cook over a very low heat for about half an hour or until tender. Stir frequently, adding a little bouillon or water if it gets too dry. When the sauerkraut is cooked add the peppercorns, bayleaf, salt and sugar. Chop the cooked meats into small pieces and add to the saucepan. Simmer for a further 10 minutes and serve.

STUFFED BELLY OF PORK

(serves 6)

3 lb. belly of pork	STUFFING
salt	1 lb. sauerkraut
1 onion	1 large cooking apple
3 tablespoons water	1 oz. butter

Ask the butcher to remove the bones from the pork. Salt it. STUFFING: Pour cold water over the sauerkraut and squeeze out the excess liquid. Peel and chop the apples finely. Mix the sauerkraut and apples with an ounce of melted butter.

Stuff the pork with this mixture and sew up with thread. Put into a meat-tin with the chopped onion. Brown in a hot oven (500°F, Mark 10) for about 15 minutes. Reduce heat (350°F, Mark 4) and add three tablespoons of water for basting. Cook for another hour and a half or until tender.

HAM WITH PRUNES OR CHERRIES

(serves 8)

3 lb. leg of ham	¾ pt water
¼ pt wine	4 bayleaves
¼ pt wine vinegar	black pepper

SAUCE
½ lb. prunes or morello cherries
4–5 lumps sugar

½ teaspoon cinnamon
¼ French loaf
knob of butter

Remove the skin from the ham. If the ham is too salty, soak it for a few hours in water. Put it in a saucepan and add the wine, wine vinegar, water, bayleaves and pepper. Cover and simmer till cooked, 20 minutes to each pound and 20 minutes over.

SAUCE: Meanwhile, cover the prunes or cherries with water and cook with the sugar and cinnamon till tender. Grate the French loaf, having removed the crusts, and fry in butter. Sieve the prunes or cherries, add the fried breadcrumbs and dilute with juice from the ham.

Pour the sauce over the ham and serve.

PORK CHOPS WITH CHERRY, APPLE OR PLUM SAUCE

(serves 6)

6 pork chops
salt, pepper
dry breadcrumbs
butter

SAUCE
3 tablespoons purée (cherry, apple or plum)

sugar or honey to taste
½ teaspoon cinnamon
2 cloves
rind of ¼ lemon
½ pt bouillon or water
3 tablespoons madeira or port

Season the chops, coat in breadcrumbs and cook in butter. They can either be fried or baked in the oven (400°F, Mark 6) for about half an hour or until tender.

SAUCE: Cook the cherries, apples or plums in a little water and sieve. Add sugar or honey, cinnamon, cloves, lemon rind, water or bouillon and madeira or port.

Pour the sauce over the chops and cook for a few minutes more.

Poultry and Game

KIEV CUTLETS

(serves 2)

1 roasting chicken (about $3\frac{1}{2}$ lb.; drawn)	salt
	butter or oil for frying
4 oz. butter	1 egg
dry breadcrumbs	$\frac{1}{2}$ lemon

Wash and dry the prepared chicken. Using a very sharp knife, cut away each breast and remove the skin. Make a slit in the middle of each breast and stuff it with the butter. This should be very hard, otherwise it will trickle out during cooking. Fold the flesh over the butter to resemble a tube. Coat in seasoned breadcrumbs, dip in beaten egg and coat in breadcrumbs again. Fry in plenty of hot butter or oil for a few minutes on each side. Garnish with slices of lemon.

This can be prepared in advance and put in the fridge to enable the butter to harden before cooking. The rest of the chicken can be minced and used for porjarski cutlets.

PORJARSKI CUTLETS

(serves 4–6)

1 chicken (about $2\frac{1}{2}$ lb.; drawn)	salt, pepper
$\frac{1}{4}$ lb. day-old French bread	dry breadcrumbs
milk or cream	butter for frying

Wash and dry the prepared bird. Remove the meat from the bones and put it through a mincer. Remove the crusts and soak the bread in milk or cream. Squeeze out the excess liquid. Put the chicken through the mincer a second time with the bread. Add the salt and pepper and mix well by hand. Form into cutlets, coat in breadcrumbs and fry in butter on both sides until cooked (about 15–20 minutes).

SPRING CHICKEN WITH GARLIC

(serves 2)

1 spring chicken (about 1½ lb.; drawn)	2 tablespoons oil
	1 tablespoon water
salt, pepper	1 sprig parsley or dill
1 clove garlic	

Wash and dry the prepared chicken and season. Cut it in half and put it in a large saucepan with the chopped garlic and olive oil and fry until brown. Add the water and parsley. Cover and simmer for about half an hour, turning from time to time. Remove and serve.

CHICKEN WITH PRUNES

(serves 4)

1 roasting chicken (about 2½ lb.; drawn)	1 sprig parsley
	1 bayleaf
salt, pepper	½ lb. prunes
2 oz. butter	1 tablespoon lemon juice
1 carrot	1–2 lumps sugar
1 stalk celery	1 tablespoon flour
1 onion	

Wash and dry the prepared chicken. Joint, season and fry the pieces lightly in butter till brown. Put them in a saucepan with the prepared vegetables, parsley and bayleaf. Add a little water, cover and stew for ¾ hour till cooked. Meanwhile, cook the prunes separately with the lemon juice and sugar in

a little water for 30–40 minutes till tender. Make a roux from
an ounce of butter and a tablespoon of flour. Gradually stir
in the prune juice and enough strained chicken bouillon to
make up half a pint. Pour the sauce over the chicken and
prunes and serve.

STUFFED GLAZED CHICKEN

(serves 4–5)

1 chicken or capon (about 5 lb.;
drawn)

STUFFING
¼ lb. fresh minced veal
2 slices stale French bread
1 oz. butter
black pepper
salt
¼ teaspoon grated nutmeg
1 egg

GLAZING
2 pts water

chicken giblets
2 carrots
1 or 2 stalks celery
1 onion or leek
1 sprig parsley
1 bayleaf
salt
5 peppercorns
1 pig's trotter or gelatine
2 lumps sugar
1 tablespoon wine vinegar or
1 sherry glass dry sherry

Wash and dry the prepared chicken or capon. Cut through
the breast bone and remove all the bones. Put the flesh back
into the skin of the chicken. Sew up where the skin has been
cut. (If you are unable to do this, the chicken can be stuffed
and glazed without removing the bones but it must not then,
of course, be put under a press when cooked.)
STUFFING: Remove the crusts and soak the bread in water.
Squeeze out the excess liquid and mix the bread with the
minced veal, melted butter, grated nutmeg, salt and pepper.
Put these ingredients through a mincer or coarse sieve. Add
the beaten egg and mix well. Stuff the bird with this mixture
and sew up.

GLAZING: Wrap the bird in a napkin and put it in a large saucepan in about 2 pts of water. Add the bones, if you have removed them, the giblets, the cleaned vegetables, the salt, peppercorns, bayleaf and parsley and the pig's trotter, if you use one. Cover and simmer for about two hours until tender.

Remove the bird when it is cooked and put it on a plate. If the bones have been removed, cover it with another plate and a 2-lb. weight and leave for about two hours. Cut the chicken in slices, or joint it if the bones have been left in, and put it in a deep serving-dish.

To make the jelly, strain the stock. If a pig's trotter has been used, brown two lumps of sugar and add them to the strained stock. Stir quickly and leave it to cool. If gelatine is used, it should be dissolved in a little water and added to the hot strained liquid. Allow 1 oz. of powdered gelatine to a pint of stock. Stir and leave to cool. When the stock has cooled, add the vinegar or sherry. When it starts to jell, pour it over the bird and leave it to set. Any remaining jelly can be chopped and used as garnish.

Serve with mayonnaise (see p. 109) or mustard sauce (see p. 108) and Russian salad (see p. 98).

CHICKEN LIVERS WITH MADEIRA SAUCE

(serves 4)

1 lb. chicken livers	SAUCE
½ pt milk	1 tablespoon flour
flour	1 oz. butter
butter	½ pt water or stock
2 onions	1 wineglass madeira
1 oz. mushrooms	
salt, pepper	

Soak the livers in milk for several hours. This whitens and

distends them. Drain and coat in flour. Peel and chop the onions and mushrooms and fry them lightly in butter. Add the livers and cook slowly for 10–15 minutes. When they are ready, put aside and keep warm.

SAUCE: Make a roux from the butter and flour and gradually add ½ pt water or stock, stirring to form a smooth sauce. Boil for several minutes, then add the madeira and simmer for 2–3 minutes, stirring continuously.

Salt and pepper the livers and put them in a deep dish with the onion and mushrooms. Pour the sauce over them and serve with rice.

TURKEY WITH APPLES AND CHERRY SAUCE
(serves 8–10)

1 turkey (trussed and drawn)	1 ½ lb. cooking apples
salt	cherry sauce using 1 lb. morello
butter	cherries (see p. 110)

Wash and dry the prepared turkey. Rub it with salt and brush with melted butter. Put it into a greased baking-tin with a little water in a hot oven (450°F, Mark 8), turning the oven down to 350°F, Mark 4 after 15 minutes when the bird starts to brown. Cook for approximately 15 minutes to each lb. and 15 minutes over, basting frequently. Potatoes can be put round the turkey to roast 1¼ hours before it is ready. A little extra butter should be added with the potatoes. Peel and core the apples and place them either inside or round the bird about ¾ hour before serving. Make the cherry sauce while the turkey is cooking. Serve with the apples, roast potatoes and cherry sauce.

TURKEY WITH LIVER STUFFING

(serves 8–10)

1 turkey (trussed and drawn)	½ small day-old French loaf
salt	2 oz. melted butter
butter	salt, black pepper
	¼ pt milk
STUFFING	2 eggs
1 lb. calf's liver	
1 turkey liver	

STUFFING: Mince the livers. Remove the crusts and grate bread. Mix the breadcrumbs with the livers and add the melted butter, milk, salt, pepper and enough beaten egg to bind.

Wash and dry the prepared turkey and rub it with salt. Stuff it with the above mixture and sew up. Put it into a greased baking-tin, brush with melted butter and cook as in the previous recipe. Serve with roast potatoes and hot red cabbage (see p. 80).

ROAST GOOSE WITH SAUERKRAUT AND APPLE SAUCE

(serves 6)

1 goose (trussed and drawn)	STUFFING
salt	1 lb. sauerkraut
¼ pt water	1 onion
apple sauce using 1½ lb. apples	1 oz. butter
(see p. 111)	3 peppercorns (optional)

STUFFING: Pour cold water over the sauerkraut and strain well. Fry the peeled and chopped onion lightly in butter and add with the peppercorns to the sauerkraut. Cover and cook slowly for about half an hour, stirring frequently. Add a little water, if necessary, to prevent it burning.

Wash and dry the prepared goose and rub it with salt. Stuff it with the sauerkraut and put it in a large baking-tin. Goose does not usually need any extra fat for cooking but add ¼ pt of water for basting. Roast as for turkey. Peeled potatoes can be put round the goose to cook 1¼ hours before serving. Serve with roast potatoes and the apple sauce.

GOOSE (Stuffed with Kasha)

(serves 6)

1 goose (trussed and drawn)	1 pt water
1 tablespoon flour	1 onion
salt	butter for frying
1½ lb. cooking apples	½ pt cooked kasha (see p. 78)
STUFFING	salt, pepper
giblets	1 sprig parsley

STUFFING: Simmer the giblets for about half an hour in a pint of salted water. Strain and reserve the liquid. Put the giblets through a mincer. Fry the peeled and chopped onion lightly in butter and mix with the giblets, kasha, salt, pepper and chopped parsley. If the stuffing is too dry add a little stock from the giblets.

Wash and dry the prepared goose and rub it with salt. Stuff it with the above mixture and sew up. Put the goose in a baking-tin and add ¼ pt of stock from the giblets for basting. Put into a hot oven (450°F, Mark 8) and reduce heat to 350°F, Mark 4 after 15 minutes when it is fairly brown and crisp. Baste frequently with the stock and cook for approximately 15 minutes to each pound and 15 minutes over. Peeled potatoes can be put in the tin to roast 1¼ hours before the goose is ready. Core the apples but do not peel them. Arrange them round the bird ¾ hour before serving. Lift out the goose, potatoes and apples when cooked. Pour off the excess fat and thicken the stock with a little flour. Serve the goose with this gravy, the apples, roast potatoes and red cabbage (see p. 80) and stuffing.

ROAST DUCK WITH MADEIRA SAUCE

(serves 4–5)

1 duck (about 5 lb.; drawn and
  trussed)
salt
2 bayleaves
6 peppercorns
1 sprig parsley
1 stalk celery
1 carrot
1 small onion

2 lb. potatoes (optional)

SAUCE
1 tablespoon flour
juice of ½ lemon or 1 tablespoon
  wine vinegar
1 wineglass madeira
½ pt stock or water

Wash and dry the prepared bird and rub it with salt. Put it into a greased baking-tin together with the bayleaves, peppercorns, chopped parsley and cleaned and chopped celery, carrot and onion. Most ducks are fat and do not need any extra fat. However, if you cook the potatoes round the duck, add some extra butter or lard. Add two tablespoons water for basting. Put into a hot oven (450°F, Mark 8) and turn down to 350°F, Mark 4, after 10–15 minutes. Allow 15 minutes to the lb. and 15 minutes over. Baste frequently. When the bird is cooked remove it from the pan and place on a dish to keep warm.

SAUCE: Pour off any excess fat and add the flour to the pan. Stir until it thickens, gradually adding ½ pt stock or water. Bring to the boil and add the lemon juice or wine vinegar. Simmer for a few minutes and add the madeira. Cover and simmer for a few more minutes. Strain and pour over the carved duck.

WILD DUCK WITH MUSHROOMS

(serves 4–6)

2 wild ducks (2–3 lb.; drawn and trussed)
salt
1–2 oz. butter (optional)

½ lb. mushrooms
butter for frying
1 tablespoon flour
salt, pepper

SAUCE
1 onion

Wash and dry the prepared birds and rub them with salt. Put them in a roasting-tin with a little water for basting and 1–2 oz. of butter, if necessary. Put into a hot oven (450°F, Mark 8) and turn down to 350°F, Mark 4, when the ducks are fairly brown and crisp. Baste frequently. Allow 15 minutes to the lb. and 15 minutes over. Twenty minutes before serving prepare the sauce.

SAUCE: Clean and chop the onion and mushrooms and fry them in a little butter until tender. Remove the ducks from the roasting-tin when cooked and put on a dish to keep warm. Thicken the juice in the tin by stirring in a tablespoon of flour. Add the onion, mushrooms, salt and pepper and more water, if required. Simmer for a few minutes.

Pour the sauce over the ducks or serve separately.

STUFFED PARTRIDGES

(serves 6)

6 partridges (drawn and trussed)
butter for frying
salt

STUFFING
1 dessertspoon chopped onion
1 small French loaf
milk
1 lb. fresh minced veal

4 egg yolks
1 oz. butter
salt, black pepper
½ teaspoon grated nutmeg

SAUCE
2 tablespoons flour
juice of 1 lemon

Wash and dry the prepared birds. Rub them with salt and fry for a few minutes in butter in a saucepan, turning them so that they brown on all sides. Remove from the pan.

STUFFING: Fry the chopped onion lightly in butter. Remove the crusts and soak the bread in milk. Squeeze out the excess liquid. Mix the onion and bread with the minced veal, egg yolks, an ounce of melted butter, salt, pepper and grated nutmeg. Stuff the birds with this mixture.

Put them back in the saucepan with a little water, cover and cook on a low heat for about 35 minutes or until tender. Joint the birds and keep them warm while you make the sauce.

SAUCE: Thicken the liquid in the saucepan with 2 tablespoons flour, adding a little more water if necessary. Stir quickly till it boils. Add the lemon juice and pour over the partridges.

GROUSE OR PARTRIDGE SOUFFLÉ

(serves 4)

2 grouse or partridge	½ teaspoon grated nutmeg
4 slices day-old French bread	4 truffles (optional)
2 oz. butter	4 large eggs
1 teaspoon salt	½ pt single cream
pepper	1 tablespoon dry breadcrumbs

Take two prepared grouse or partridges. Wash and dry the birds with a towel. Remove all the flesh from the bones with a sharp knife. Remove the crusts and soak the bread in water. Squeeze out the excess liquid. Put the meat and the bread through a mincer and mix them with an ounce of melted butter, salt, pepper, nutmeg, chopped truffles and the egg yolks and cream. Blend well. Beat the egg whites until they stand in peaks and fold them into the mixture. Transfer to a large buttered soufflé-dish and sprinkle with breadcrumbs. Put in a fairly hot oven (400°F, Mark 6) for about 35 minutes until brown and risen. Alternatively, cover with buttered greaseproof paper, tie round with string and steam for 40–45 minutes.

ROAST PHEASANT

(serves 4)

1 pheasant (trussed and drawn)	2 slices streaky bacon
salt	1 tablespoon dry breadcrumbs
bacon fat or lard	2 lb. potatoes
1½ oz. butter	flour

Wash and dry the prepared pheasant. Rub with salt and bacon fat or lard. Put a knob of butter inside the bird as pheasants are inclined to be dry. Tie the bacon round the breast and put the bird in a greased baking-tin surrounded by the peeled potatoes. Add two or three tablespoons of water for basting. Put into a hot oven (450°F, Mark 8) and turn it down to 350°F, Mark 4 after about 10 minutes. Cook 15 minutes to the lb. and 15 minutes over. When the pheasant is almost cooked, pour two tablespoons of melted butter over it and coat in breadcrumbs. Brown for a few minutes longer and transfer to a serving-dish with the potatoes and keep warm. Add a little water to the fat in the tin and thicken with a little flour. Warm through. Serve the pheasant with the gravy, potatoes and red cabbage. The tail feathers can be stuck in the bird for decoration.

Alternatively, the pheasant may be cooked on a spit. To prevent it drying too much, cut small slits in the bird and insert small pieces of bacon fat or lard in them. Salt the inside well and put on a spit to cook. When nearly ready, coat in breadcrumbs and brown for a few minutes longer.

WOODCOCK

(serves 4)

4 woodcocks (drawn and trussed)
salt
5 oz. butter
8 slices streaky bacon

3 oz. melted butter
salt, pepper
juice of 1 lemon

STUFFING
4 oz. white breadcrumbs

Take 4 prepared woodcocks. Wash and dry them and rub with salt. Melt 5 oz. butter in a saucepan and brown the birds on all sides.

STUFFING: Mix the breadcrumbs with the lemon juice, melted butter and a little salt and pepper. Stuff the birds with this mixture.

Tie two pieces of streaky bacon round the breast of each bird. Put the birds in a baking-tin. Reheat the butter left in the saucepan and pour it over the birds. Put in a hot oven (450°F, Mark 8), reducing heat to 350°F, Mark 4 after 10 minutes. Baste frequently and cook for about 30 minutes or until tender. Serve with cherry sauce (see p. 110) or hot red cabbage (see p. 80). The birds can also be cooked on a spit.

Vegetables

POTATO CUTLETS

(serves 6)

2 lb. potatoes	dry breadcrumbs
salt and pepper	butter or oil for frying
3 eggs	1 sprig parsley
1 oz. butter	1 pt mushroom sauce (see p. 107)
1½ oz. flour	

Wash the potatoes and boil them in their skins in salted water until ready. Peel them and put through a sieve. Mash with the butter. Add two beaten eggs, flour, salt and pepper and form into rissoles. Dip in beaten egg, coat in breadcrumbs and fry for a few minutes on each side. Garnish with parsley and serve with mushroom sauce.

POTATOES WITH MUSHROOM SAUCE

(serves 6)

3 lb. potatoes	1 onion
salt	2 tablespoons butter
1 sprig parsley or dill	1 teaspoon flour
	¼ pt. fresh or sour cream
SAUCE	
¾ lb. mushrooms	

SAUCE: Clean and chop the mushrooms. Peel the onion and chop finely. Fry the mushrooms and onion in butter for about 20 minutes. Season. Stir in the flour, cook for a few minutes and add the cream.

Meanwhile, wash the potatoes and boil them in their skins in salted water until they are cooked. They should be ready at the same time as the sauce. Peel and slice. Pour the sauce over the potatoes and garnish with chopped dill or parsley.

POTATOES WITH SOUR CREAM (1)

(serves 4)

1 ½ lb. potatoes
salt and pepper
1 oz. butter

⅓ pt sour cream
1 oz. grated cheese (optional)
1 sprig parsley

Peel the potatoes and boil them in salted water until they are cooked. Strain and slice them and arrange them in layers in a buttered fireproof dish. Add salt and pepper to the sour cream and pour it over the potatoes. Dot with butter and sprinkle with grated cheese. Bake in a fairly hot oven (400°F, Mark 6) for about 20 minutes or until brown. Garnish with chopped parsley before serving.

POTATOES WITH SOUR CREAM (2)

(serves 6)

2 lb. new potatoes
salt

¼ pt sour cream
1 sprig dill

Wash the potatoes and boil them in salted water until cooked. Peel. Strain off any excess water and return them to the saucepan. Add the sour cream. Warm through and serve garnished with chopped dill.

KASHA (Buckwheat)

Kasha is part of the staple Russian diet and when well cooked is a delicious accompaniment to lamb, pork or goose. It is traditionally served with borshch and shchi.

Use two parts water to one part kasha when cooking. The kasha will increase in bulk like rice when cooked. Pick over the kasha to remove any husks and cook in one of the following ways:

1. Roast the kasha in a frying-pan without fat, stirring all the time with a wooden spoon until it starts to pop. Transfer to a fireproof dish, allowing plenty of space for the kasha to increase in bulk. Add boiling water and salt. Put plenty of butter on top as this will soak in. Cover with a lid and bake in a moderate oven (350°F, Mark 4) for 40–45 minutes. Dark hard grains will form on top. Serve with plenty of butter.

2. Roast the kasha in a frying-pan as above. Add the boiling water and salt and cook in a double saucepan on top of the stove for about 45 minutes.

SAUERKRAUT

(serves 6)

2 lb. *sauerkraut*	1 lb. *cooking apples*
¼ lb. *butter*	*strawberry or apple juice (optional)*

If the sauerkraut is very sour pour cold water over it and squeeze out the excess liquid. Melt the butter in a saucepan and add the sauerkraut and the peeled, cored and chopped apples. Cover and simmer for 30–40 minutes, stirring frequently. A little strawberry or apple juice can be added, if available. Otherwise a little stock or water may be necessary to keep it moist during cooking.

Serve with goose, duck, pork or veal.

RUSSIAN CABBAGE

(serves 6)

1 large white Dutch cabbage	salt and pepper
8 oz. dry white breadcrumbs	1 ½ pts single cream
¼ lb. butter	

Discard the outer leaves and wash the cabbage well. Scoop out the centre and chop fairly finely. Mix the chopped cabbage with the breadcrumbs and fill the cabbage with this mixture. Put the cabbage and any of the left-over mixture in a large saucepan. Cut the butter into cubes and put it on top of the cabbage. Pour in the cream. Season. Cover and simmer for 1–1 ½ hours until tender.

RED CABBAGE

(serves 6)

1 red cabbage	1 large cooking apple
1 teaspoon salt	1 tablespoon sugar
pepper	2 tablespoons lemon juice or wine
1 oz. butter	vinegar

Discard the outer leaves and cut out any thick veins. Wash the cabbage, shred and put in a saucepan. Cover with boiling water and leave to stand for about 20 minutes. Strain and add salt. Melt the butter in a saucepan. Add the cabbage and stir well. Peel, core and slice the apple and add it to the cabbage. Cover and cook slowly for about 30 minutes, stirring from time to time. The cabbage should remain moist, otherwise it will burn. Before serving, adjust the seasoning and add the sugar and lemon juice or vinegar.

CAULIFLOWER WITH BUTTER AND BREADCRUMBS

(serves 4)

1 medium cauliflower	2 oz. salted butter
1 teaspoon salt	1 tablespoon dry breadcrumbs

Wash the cauliflower and put it in boiling salted water in a saucepan. Cover and simmer for about 20 minutes until cooked. Transfer to a warm dish. A few minutes before the cauliflower is ready melt the butter in a small saucepan. Add the breadcrumbs and cook gently for a few minutes until the breadcrumbs have absorbed the butter. Serve with the cauliflower.

CHESTNUT PURÉE

(serves 4)

½ lb. chestnuts	pinch of salt
⅓ pt milk	1 oz. butter
1 teaspoon sugar	¼ pt double cream

Cut the ends off the chestnuts with a sharp knife. Simmer in salted water in a saucepan with the lid on, for about 20 minutes until soft. Remove the shells and any hard skin. Cut into pieces and put into a saucepan with the milk, sugar and salt. Cook gently for a further 10–15 minutes until soft enough to mash. Put through a sieve with the milk. Add the butter and cream. Heat through, mixing thoroughly. Serve with roast beef or turkey.

Sweet Corn

Preparation and cooking: Only young cobs are suitable for

boiling. They can be cooked with or without the leaves. Wash and simmer for 15–20 minutes in salted water until tender. Be careful not to overcook. Serve with butter or white sauce (see p. 105).

SWEET CORN WITH SOUR CREAM

(serves 3–4)

3 corn cobs	1 oz. butter
3 tablespoons sour cream	parsley
1 oz. grated cheddar or gruyère cheese	

Cook the sweet corn as above. Remove the grains from the cobs and mix them with the sour cream. Put into a buttered fireproof dish, sprinkle with cheese and dot with butter. Cook in a moderate oven (350°F, Mark 4) for about 15 minutes or until brown. Garnish with chopped parsley.

Asparagus

Preparation and cooking: Cut off the hard end of the stalk with a sharp knife. Scrape or peel the white part. Wash, drain and tie in bundles of 8 to 10. Cook, lying flat, in boiling salted water in a saucepan with a large base. Simmer, with the lid on, for 20–25 minutes, according to size. Be careful not to overcook. When tender, transfer to a warm plate and serve with hollandaise sauce (see p. 106).

ASPARAGUS

(serves 4)

½ lb. asparagus	1 oz. butter
salt	1½ oz. cheddar or gruyère cheese
½ pt white sauce (see p. 105)	

Prepare asparagus as above. Cut into 2-in. lengths and boil in salted water until tender. Meanwhile, prepare the white sauce. Butter a fireproof dish and pour in half the sauce. Lay the asparagus carefully in the dish and cover with the rest of the sauce. Grate the cheese and sprinkle on top. Dot with knobs of butter and bake in a fairly hot oven (400°F, Mark 6) for 15 minutes or until brown or, alternatively, brown for a few minutes under the grill.

Serve as a separate course or with roast beef or cotletti (see p. 52).

Beetroot

Preparation and cooking: Wash the beetroot carefully, making sure that the skin is not damaged or cut in any way as this will cause the beetroot to 'bleed' or lose colour. Leave about 1–2 in. of the top on until the beetroot is cooked.
BOILING: Cover with boiling salted water and simmer gently with the lid on for about an hour. The cooking time will, of course, depend on the size and age of the beetroot. If the beetroot is to be used for salad, leave in the water to cool before peeling off the skin.
BAKING: Young beetroots are especially good baked as this method retains all the juice and flavour. Wrap the beetroot in greased paper or aluminium foil and bake in a moderate oven (350°F, Mark 4) for about an hour, depending on size and age.

BEETROOT WITH SOUR CREAM
(serves 4)

1 lb. raw beetroot	salt
knob of butter	1 teaspoon sugar
1 teaspoon vinegar	¼ pt sour cream
1 dessertspoon flour	

Peel and wash the beetroot. Slice them and cut into thin strips. Put into a saucepan with the butter, vinegar and enough water to prevent them catching. Cover and simmer for about 40 minutes until tender. Stir in the flour, salt and sugar. Add the sour cream. Bring to the boil and serve.

BEANS WITH BEETROOT IN SOUR CREAM
(serves 6)

½ lb. beans (kidney, butter or flageolets)	⅓ pt water
salt	1 teaspoon sugar
½ lb. raw beetroot	1 teaspoon vinegar
1 oz. melted butter	2 tablespoons sour cream
	parsley

BEANS: Soak the beans overnight in cold water. Discard the water and transfer the beans to a saucepan. Cover with fresh cold salted water and simmer with the lid on for about an hour or until the beans are tender.

BEETROOT: Peel the beetroot and cut it into small cubes. Put it in a saucepan with the melted butter, water and salt about 20 minutes after the beans so that they are both ready at the same time. Cover and simmer for about 30–40 minutes until cooked. Add the sugar and vinegar and mix thoroughly. (Ready-cooked beetroot can be used. If so, peel, cut into cubes and heat through in the butter. Add sugar, salt and vinegar.)

Mix the strained beans with the beetroot. Add the sour cream and warm through if it is to be served hot. Garnish with parsley. Serve hot or cold with any type of meat.

SWEDES IN WHITE SAUCE
(serves 6)

1½ lb. swedes	1 pt white sauce (see p. 105)
salt	

Wash and peel the swedes and cut them into cubes. Boil them in salted water for about 30 minutes until almost cooked. Pour off the liquid and use to make the white sauce: one part vegetable stock to one part milk. Cook the sauce for a few minutes. Add the swedes and cook for a further five minutes or so.

Carrots can be cooked in this way, in which case they should be peeled and sliced thinly.

TURNIPS IN CREAM

(serves 3)

½ lb. turnips
salt
½ oz. butter

4 tablespoons double cream
1 teaspoon sugar

Peel the turnips and cut into cubes or strips. Boil in salted water for about 30 minutes until tender. Strain. Melt the butter in a saucepan. Add the turnips, cream, sugar and a little salt. Stir until heated through. Serve with roast meat.

This can also be made with carrots. Young carrots will only need scraping and can be cooked whole.

PUMPKIN IN SOUR CREAM

(serves 6)

1 lb. pumpkin
½ teaspoon salt
1 tablespoon flour

2 oz. butter
3 tablespoons sour cream
1 teaspoon sugar

Peel the pumpkin and remove the seeds. Slice thinly, salt and coat lightly in flour. Fry in butter till golden brown. Test with a fork to see if the pumpkin is tender. Add the sour cream and sugar and heat through.

Serve with roast veal or chicken.

CELERY IN SOUR CREAM

(serves 4)

1 large head celery
salt
1 sprig dill or parsley

SAUCE
¼ onion

½ oz. butter
1 teaspoon tomato purée
3–4 tablespoons sour cream
salt and pepper

Cut off the leaves, trim the root and scrape the outer stalks of the celery clean. Cut into four and wash thoroughly. Tie together in small bundles with cotton. Put into a saucepan in salted water, cover and simmer for about an hour until tender. About five minutes before serving prepare the sauce.
SAUCE: Peel the onion and chop it very finely. Fry in butter till golden brown. Add the tomato purée, the sour cream and a little salt and pepper and warm through.

Strain the celery, remove the cotton and transfer to a warm serving-dish. Pour over the sauce and garnish with chopped dill or parsley.

CUCUMBER IN SOUR CREAM

(serves 4)

½ large fresh cucumber
salt and pepper
1 tablespoon flour

butter or butter and oil for cooking
1 egg
3 tablespoons sour cream

Peel the cucumber and divide it lengthways and across. Sprinkle with salt and pepper and coat in flour. Fry gently in butter or oil until brown and transfer to a buttered fireproof dish. Mix the sour cream with the egg and pour it over the cucumber. Bake in a moderate oven (350°F, Mark 4) for about 15 minutes. Serve as a separate dish or with roast meat.

UKRAINIAN STEWED VEGETABLES

(serves 8)

1 onion	1 large aubergine
3 tablespoons olive oil	1 teaspoon sugar
½ lb. carrots	salt to taste
1 lb. tomatoes	2 teaspoons lemon juice
2 green peppers	

Peel the onion and chop fairly finely. Fry very slowly in oil for about five minutes taking care not to let it brown. Peel the carrots and slice them, if young, or dice if old. Add them to the onion and cook slowly for a further five minutes. Peel and quarter the tomatoes. Remove the stalk and all the seeds from the peppers and cut them into fairly small pieces. Top and tail the aubergine and cut into large pieces. Add the tomatoes, peppers and aubergine to the onion and carrots. Cover and cook slowly for about 40 minutes until the carrots are tender, stirring frequently. Ten minutes before serving add the sugar, salt and lemon juice. Serve hot or cold.

POTATOES STUFFED WITH MUSHROOMS

(serves 6)

1 2 large potatoes	1 leek
salt	butter for frying
¼ lb. melted butter	½ small stale French loaf
	1 egg
STUFFING	salt and black pepper
½ lb. mushrooms	

STUFFING: Wash the mushrooms and leek. Chop them finely and fry lightly in butter for about 20 minutes. Remove the crusts and grate the bread. Mix with the cooked leek and mushrooms. Add the beaten egg and season the mixture.

Peel and wash the potatoes and boil them for a few

minutes in salted water. Cut off the tops and scoop out the centres. Fill with the stuffing and replace the tops. Transfer to a large saucepan or casserole. Sprinkle with salt and pour over the melted butter. Cover the saucepan and cook gently on top of the oven or put into a hot oven (450°F, Mark 8), turning down (350°F, Mark 4) after about half an hour. Baste frequently. The potatoes should take about an hour to cook. If baked in the oven, remove the lid for the last 20 minutes to allow them to brown.

POTATOES STUFFED WITH MEAT

(serves 4)

8 large potatoes	STUFFING
salt	1 lb. raw minced beef
butter or fat for cooking	1 onion
1 lb. tomatoes	oil for frying
2 tablespoons sour cream	salt

STUFFING: Peel and chop the onion and fry it lightly for a few minutes. Add the minced beef and cook for about 20 minutes until brown. Season.

Peel and wash the potatoes and boil them for a few minutes in salted water. Cut the tops off and scoop out the centres. Fill the potatoes with the stuffing and replace the tops. Transfer the potatoes to a greased baking-tin, add a knob of butter to each potato and cook in a moderate oven (350°F, Mark 4) for about half an hour. Wash and slice the tomatoes and put them in the tin with the potatoes. Cook for a further 20 minutes or until the potatoes are ready, basting from time to time. Remove the potatoes and keep them warm. Sieve the tomatoes and juice from the tin, adding a little water. Adjust the seasoning and stir in two tablespoons of sour cream. Heat through and pour over the potatoes.

GREEN PEPPERS STUFFED WITH VEGETABLES

(serves 6)

6 green peppers
salt
1 lb. ripe tomatoes
lemon juice to taste
sugar to taste

STUFFING
6 carrots

1 stick celery
½ small swede
½ small turnip
1 large onion
1 sprig parsley
oil for frying

STUFFING: Peel and wash all the vegetables. Chop them finely and fry lightly in oil, taking care not to brown them.

Wash the peppers, cut off the tops and make sure that all the seeds are removed as these give a very bitter taste. Fill the peppers with the stuffing and put them, together with any left-over vegetables, in a large saucepan or greased casserole. Add salt. Meanwhile, cook the tomatoes in a little salted water for a few minutes. Strain and sieve. Pour the tomato sauce over the peppers and either cover and simmer on top of the stove or cook in a moderate oven (350°F, Mark 4) for about an hour. Before serving, adjust the seasoning and add a little lemon juice and sugar to taste. This dish may be served hot or cold.

GREEN PEPPERS WITH MINCED BEEF

(serves 4)

8 green peppers
1 lb. ripe tomatoes or 2–3
  tablespoons tomato purée
1 teaspoon cornflour (optional)
2 tablespoons sour cream

STUFFING
1 lb. raw minced beef

1 onion
1 tablespoon cooked rice
salt
oil or butter for frying

STUFFING: Peel the onion and chop finely. Fry lightly in butter or oil. Add the minced meat and cook for a further 20 minutes, adding a little water if it gets too dry. Mix with the cooked rice and salt to taste.

Cut the tops off the peppers and make sure that all the seeds are scooped out. Stuff the peppers with the above mixture and put them into a saucepan or greased casserole-dish. Meanwhile, cook the tomatoes separately in a little salted water and sieve when ready. If tomato purée is used instead dilute it with about ¾ pt water. The tomato sauce can be thickened with a teaspoon of cornflour mixed with a little water. Pour the sauce over the peppers. Cover the saucepan and simmer for about an hour or bake in a moderate oven (350°F, Mark 4). When ready, add the sour cream to the sauce and warm through.

AUBERGINES WITH VEGETABLE STUFFING

(serves 3)

3 aubergines	2 sticks celery
salt	½ parsnip or turnip
oil for cooking	1 onion
1 lb. tomatoes	1 sprig parsley
sugar to taste	oil for cooking
lemon juice to taste	

STUFFING
2 carrots

Cut the ends off the aubergines and remove the centre part. Rub well with salt both inside and out.
STUFFING: Clean and chop the vegetables finely. Cook them slowly in oil, with the parsley, for about 10 minutes. Do not allow them to brown. Stuff the aubergines with this mixture.

Put the stuffed aubergines into a saucepan with a little

more oil and salt. Cook the tomatoes in a little salted water for a few minutes. Strain and sieve and add to the aubergines. Cover and simmer for 30–40 minutes until the aubergines are tender. Before serving, add a little sugar and lemon juice to the sauce and more salt, if necessary. Serve hot or cold.

AUBERGINES STUFFED WITH BEEF OR CHICKEN
(serves 4)

4 aubergines
salt
¼ pt sour cream

2 tablespoons breadcrumbs
1 egg
salt and pepper

STUFFING
½ lb. finely minced raw beef or
  chicken

Slice the ends off the aubergines, remove the centre part and salt both inside and out.

STUFFING: Mix the finely minced beef or chicken with the beaten egg, breadcrumbs and salt and pepper.

Stuff the aubergines with the mixture and put them in a well-greased casserole in a moderate oven (350°F, Mark 4) for about an hour until ready. Pour over the sour cream five minutes before serving.

STUFFED MARROW
(serves 4)

1 medium-sized marrow
oil or butter for cooking
1 pt tomato sauce (see p. 106)
2 tablespoons sour cream

oil or butter for cooking
1 lb. fresh minced beef
salt and pepper
1 tablespoon rice

STUFFING
1 large onion

STUFFING: Fry the finely chopped onion. Add the minced beef and fry for about 20 minutes until brown. Add salt and pepper. Meanwhile, boil the rice in salted water until cooked. Strain and add to the mince.

Peel the marrow, cut it in half and remove all the seeds. Fill with the stuffing and tie the halves together again with cotton. Put the marrow in a greased baking-tin with plenty of oil or butter and bake in a moderate oven (350°F, Mark 4) for about an hour or until ready. Baste frequently. Prepare the tomato sauce while the marrow is cooking. Pour the sauce over the marrow and then the sour cream on top a few minutes before serving.

BAKED STUFFED ONIONS

(serves 4)

4 Spanish onions	2 oz. calf's liver
salt and pepper	salt and pepper
butter for cooking	½ oz. butter
1 tablespoon dry breadcrumbs	¼ teaspoon grated nutmeg
½ oz. butter	

STUFFING
2 oz. streaky bacon

Choose onions of equal size. Peel them and cut off the tops with a sharp knife. Scoop out the centres carefully and salt and pepper the insides.

STUFFING: Cut off the rind and chop the bacon. Wash the liver, removing any skin or membrane and chop, together with a little of the onion cut out from the centres. Add to the bacon. Season and fry lightly in butter for 5–10 minutes. Put through a mincer, add the nutmeg and mix together thoroughly.

Stuff the onions and tie them securely with cotton. Put

them in a large saucepan in a little boiling salted water. Cover and cook for about 10–15 minutes. Grease a baking-tin and carefully transfer the onions. Sprinkle with bread-crumbs, dot with butter and cook in a moderate oven (350°F, Mark 4) for about an hour or until ready. Serve as a separate course.

Salads

CUCUMBER SALAD WITH SOUR CREAM
(serves 4)

1 fresh cucumber
salt

¼ pt sour cream sauce (see p. 109)
2 sprigs dill or parsley

Wash and peel the cucumber. Slice thinly and salt. Leave to stand for a few minutes. Add the sour cream sauce and garnish with chopped dill or parsley. Chill for a few minutes and serve.

TOMATO SALAD WITH ONION AND GREEN PEPPER
(serves 3)

1 lb. tomatoes
¼ Spanish onion
½ green pepper

French dressing (see p. 110)
salt (optional)

Slice the tomatoes and peel and slice the onion finely. Remove the seeds from the green pepper and chop into fairly small pieces. Pour the dressing over the tomatoes, onion and pepper and toss. A little extra salt can be added, if necessary.

KIDNEY BEAN SALAD
(serves 4)

½ lb. kidney beans
sprig parsley
salt, pepper

1 small onion
2 tablespoons olive oil
1 tablespoon lemon or gooseberry juice

Soak the beans overnight in cold water. Cook in salted water with the onion and parsley for about an hour until tender. Drain. Put into a bowl and add pepper, oil, lemon or gooseberry juice and more salt, if necessary. Serve with cold mutton. This salad can be made with small red or white haricot beans or flageolets.

SPRING SALAD

(serves 4–6)

1 lettuce
1 boiled new carrot
2 tomatoes
2–3 boiled new potatoes
1 bunch of radishes

½ fresh cucumber
2 hard-boiled eggs
2 spring onions
sour cream sauce (see p. 109)

Wash the fresh vegetables. Strain the lettuce, pat dry and tear into small pieces. Put into the middle of a large salad bowl. Slice the carrot, tomatoes, potatoes, radishes and cucumber and arrange round the lettuce. Garnish with slices of egg and finely chopped spring onions. Serve the sour cream sauce with the salad.

RED CABBAGE SALAD

(serves 6–8)

1 lb. red cabbage
1 teaspoon cooking salt

French dressing (see p. 110)
2 teaspoons sugar

Wash the cabbage and remove the outer leaves, thick stems and veins. Cut into strips and rub the cooking salt in well. Leave for an hour. Drain off the liquid. Add the French dressing with two teaspoons of sugar and mix well.

RADISH SALAD

(serves 3–4)

2 bunches of radishes
salt, pepper

1 hard-boiled egg
sour cream sauce (see p. 109)

Wash and top-and-tail the radishes and cut them into thin slices. Add salt and pepper. Put the egg yolk through a sieve and mix it with the sour cream sauce. Pour the sauce over the radishes and mix well. Garnish with chopped egg-whites. Chill and serve.

CAUCASIAN SALAD

(serves 3–4)

1 bunch of radishes
½ fresh cucumber
2 spring onions
salt, pepper

3 tablespoons sour milk or yoghurt
pinch of sugar (optional)
1 sprig dill

Wash and top-and-tail the radishes and slice them thinly. Cut the cucumber in thin slices. Clean the spring onions and chop them finely. Season. Add the sour milk or yoghurt and a pinch of sugar. Mix all the ingredients thoroughly. Garnish with chopped dill and chill for half an hour before serving.

BEETROOT SALAD

(serves 4)

1 lb. cooked beetroot
2 tablespoons olive oil
3 tablespoons wine vinegar

1 teaspoon sugar
salt
1 sprig dill or parsley

Peel and slice the beetroot and cut into thin strips. Mix

T – R.C. – D

the oil, vinegar, sugar and salt and pour over the beetroot. Mix well and leave to stand for about half an hour before serving. Garnish with chopped dill or parsley.

RUSSIAN SALAD

(serves 4)

1 lb. boiled potatoes
1 salted or pickled cucumber
1 cooked carrot
½ lb. cooked beetroot

1 teaspoon finely chopped onion (optional)
1 tablespoon cooked green peas
French dressing (see p. 110)

Slice the potatoes and slice and quarter the cucumber and carrot. Cut the beetroot into cubes. Put them in a bowl together with the onion and peas. Pour over the French dressing and mix well. Chill before serving.

SAUERKRAUT AND CRANBERRY SALAD

(serves 6)

1 lb. sauerkraut
1 tablespoon olive oil
1 tablespoon sugar

1 eating apple
2 stalks celery (optional)
¼ lb. cranberries

If the sauerkraut is very sour, pour cold water over it and squeeze out the liquid. Add the oil and sugar to the sauerkraut. Peel, core and chop the apple and clean the celery and cut it into strips. Wash the cranberries. Add the apple, celery and cranberries to the sauerkraut and mix well. This salad is particularly good with cold poultry or cold roast pork.

HERRING SALAD

(serves 6)

2 salted herring fillets	2 hard-boiled eggs
2 large cooked potatoes	1 teaspoon made mustard
1 salted cucumber	salt
1 eating apple	3 tablespoons olive oil
¼ lb. cooked beetroot	2 tablespoons vinegar
1 small onion	2 stalks dill or parsley

Cut the herring fillets into pieces about an inch long. Slice the potatoes and cucumber and cut the slices in half. Peel and core the apple, peel the beetroot and cut them both into strips. Peel the onion and chop finely. Put all the ingredients into a bowl, keeping aside a little beetroot for decoration.

Mix the egg yolks with the mustard and salt. Blend the oil in gradually and add the vinegar. Mix well and add to the other ingredients. Garnish with chopped egg-white, strips of beetroot and chopped dill or parsley.

COD SALAD WITH HORSERADISH

(serves 6)

1 lb. cooked fillet of cod	salt
½ fresh cucumber	2 teaspoons wine vinegar
½ lb. cooked potatoes	2 spring onions
1 oz. grated horseradish	1 sprig parsley
¼ pt mayonnaise (see p. 109)	

Remove the skin and cut the boiled cod into small pieces. Peel and slice the cucumber and slice the potatoes. Put most of the grated horseradish in a bowl. Add the mayonnaise, vinegar, and salt. Mix in the fish, potatoes and most of the cucumber and transfer to a salad bowl. Garnish with pieces of cucumber, chopped spring onion, grated horseradish and parsley.

RICE SALAD

(serves 6)

6 oz. rice
salt
¼ pt. French dressing (see p. 110)
2 cooked carrots

1 tablespoon cooked green peas
2 sprigs parsley
1 dessertspoon sultanas (optional)
1 tablespoon chopped red or green pepper

Boil the rice in salted water. Transfer to a sieve and run cold water through. Put in a bowl and pour over the French dressing. Chop the carrots into small cubes. Add the carrots, peas, chopped parsley, pepper and sultanas to the rice. Serve with cold meat.

POTATO SALAD

(serves 4–5)

1 lb. boiled potatoes
2 spring onions
½ teaspoon made mustard

French dressing (see p. 110) or mayonnaise (see p. 109)
1 sprig dill or parsley

Slice the cooked potatoes and put them in a bowl with the finely chopped spring onions, the mustard and the French dressing or mayonnaise. Mix. The flavour is improved if the dressing is added while the potatoes are still hot. Garnish with chopped dill or parsley.

CELERY AND PINEAPPLE SALAD

(serves 4)

¼ lb. fresh pineapple
2–3 stalks celery
2 tablespoons French dressing (see
  p. 110)

1 teaspoon sugar
½ lettuce
2 slices cooked beetroot

Remove the skin from the pineapple and wash and trim celery. Cut them both into thin strips and mix with a tablespoon of the French dressing and the sugar.

Wash the lettuce, drain and pat dry. Tear into small pieces and arrange in a salad bowl. Put the celery and pineapple round the edge. Cut the beetroot into cubes and place in the centre. Pour the rest of the French dressing over the salad. Serve with cold meat or poultry.

If tinned pineapple is substituted for fresh the sugar should be omitted.

CHICORY AND FRUIT SALAD

(serves 3–4)

2 heads of chicory
1 orange
1 apple or banana
grated lemon or orange rind

2 tablespoons mayonnaise or
mayonnaise with sour cream
(see p. 109)

Remove the outer leaves of the chicory, cut off the base, wash and slice. Peel the orange, slice thinly and remove the pips. Peel and core the apple or peel the banana and cut in fine slices. Mix all the ingredients with the mayonnaise and garnish with coarsely grated lemon or orange rind.

Serve with cold meat or poultry.

BEAN AND ASPARAGUS SALAD

(serves 4)

2 oz. runner beans
2 oz. asparagus
1 tablespoon green peas
2 oz. cauliflower
salt, pepper
½ lettuce

1 tomato
¼ fresh cucumber
2 tablespoons French dressing (see
   p. 110) or mayonnaise with sour
   cream (see p. 109)
1 sprig parsley or dill

Top-and-tail the beans and string them. Remove the hard ends from the asparagus and cut into inch-long pieces. Wash the beans, asparagus, peas and cauliflower and boil them in salted water, with the lid on, for 20 minutes or till cooked. Leave them to cool in the water they have been cooked in. When cool, drain, divide the cauliflower into flowerlets and slice the beans. Wash and divide the lettuce. Pat dry and tear into small pieces. Peel and slice the tomato and cucumber. Mix all the vegetables in a bowl, season and add the French dressing or mayonnaise with sour cream. Garnish with chopped parsley or dill.

KAZAN SALAD

(serves 6)

4–6 oz. cold roast beef
4 oz. cooked potato
1 salted or pickled cucumber
1 cooked carrot
1 tablespoon cooked peas
½ lettuce

2–3 tablespoons mayonnaise (see
   p. 109) or mayonnaise with
   sour cream (see p. 109)
1 hard-boiled egg
1 eating apple
1 sprig parsley or dill

Cut the beef, potato, cucumber and carrot into small, thin slices. Add the green peas and mix well with the mayonnaise. Wash the lettuce, drain and pat dry. Slice the egg and peel, core and slice the apple. Chop the dill or parsley. Tear the lettuce into small pieces and arrange in a bowl. Put the dressed meat salad in the middle. Garnish with the egg, apple and parsley or dill.

FRUIT SALAD WITH MAYONNAISE

(serves 4)

3 eating apples	1 teaspoon sugar
1 pear	pinch of salt
1 orange	4 tablespoons mayonnaise (see p. 109)
1 mandarin	juice of ¼ lemon

Peel and slice the fruit, discarding the cores and pips where necessary. Put in a bowl and sprinkle with sugar and salt. Add the mayonnaise mixed with lemon juice. Garnish with grated orange rind. Grapes, blackcurrants, redcurrants or cooked prunes can also be used for decoration.

Serve with hot or cold meat, poultry or game.

Sauces

BASIC WHITE SAUCE

1 oz. butter
1 oz. flour

1 pt milk
salt, pepper

Melt the butter in a saucepan. Stir in the flour. Mix well
and cook gently for 1–2 minutes. Remove from the heat and
gradually add the milk, which may be warm, stirring to
obtain a smooth consistency. Return to the heat, season and
cook gently for about five minutes.

CAPER SAUCE

1 oz. butter
1 oz. flour
1 pt milk

salt
2 tablespoons capers

Make a white sauce as in the previous recipe and add a
few capers.

PICKLED MUSHROOM SAUCE

1 oz. butter
1 oz. flour
1 pt milk

salt, pepper
6 small pickled mushrooms

Make a white sauce and add salt, pepper and the finely
chopped pickled mushrooms. This sauce is served with fried
fish cutlets.

TOMATO SAUCE

½ onion
½ oz. butter
2 teaspoons flour
¾ lb. ripe tomatoes or 3 tablespoons
  tomato purée

½ pt water
1 teaspoon sugar
lemon juice or wine vinegar to taste
½ teaspoon salt

Peel and chop the onion and fry it lightly in butter. Stir in the flour. Then add the water and tomatoes and simmer slowly for about 30 minutes. If tomato purée is used, double the amount of water will be necessary, but it will only need a few minutes cooking. Sieve and add sugar and lemon juice or vinegar and salt.

TOMATO SAUCE WITH CAPERS OR PICKLED MUSHROOMS

Make basic tomato sauce (see above) substituting either two tablespoons of capers or a few pickled mushrooms for the lemon juice or vinegar.

HOLLANDAISE SAUCE

3 tablespoons lemon juice
salt
6 peppercorns
3 egg yolks

2 tablespoons water or stock
  (chicken or fish)
4 oz. butter

Put the lemon juice, peppercorns, salt and water into a small pan and heat till reduced to 2 dessertspoons of liquid. Strain and put in a double saucepan. Stir the egg yolks in gradually and then add the softened butter in small pieces, stirring all the time until it thickens. Season delicately.

WHITE WINE SAUCE

1 medium onion	1 egg yolk
1 sprig chopped parsley	salt
2 oz. butter	2 tablespoons dry white wine
1 oz. flour	squeeze of lemon juice
1 pt fish stock	

Peel and chop the onion and fry the onion and parsley lightly in half the butter. Stir in the flour to make a roux. Gradually add a pint of hot fish stock, stirring all the time. Simmer for several minutes and take off the heat. Blend in the egg yolk and the rest of the butter. Add salt and sieve. Add the wine and lemon juice. Heat through, being careful not to let it boil. Serve this sauce with fish katushki.

MUSHROOM SAUCE

½ lb. mushrooms	salt, pepper
1 onion	1 dessertspoon flour
butter for frying	1 cup fresh or sour cream

Clean and chop the mushrooms and stalks. Chop the onion finely and brown it lightly in butter. Add the chopped mushrooms and cook over a low heat for about 20 minutes. Add salt, pepper and flour and stir well. Add the sour cream and heat through. Serve with meat, fish or potato cutlets and kasha.

MUSHROOM SAUCE WITH WINE

½ lb. mushrooms	¼ pt water
1 oz. butter	salt, pepper
juice of ¼ lemon	1 teaspoon sugar
3 tablespoons water or bouillon	1–2 wineglasses dry white wine
1 dessertspoon flour	2 egg yolks

Clean the mushrooms, including the stalks, and cut into fairly large pieces. Stew gently in a saucepan in ½ oz. of melted butter for a few minutes. Add the lemon juice and 3 tablespoons water or bouillon and simmer for about 20 minutes until soft. In a separate saucepan make a roux from a dessertspoon of flour and half an ounce of butter. Do not let it brown. Gradually add ¼ pt water, salt, pepper and sugar. Stir in the wine and bring to the boil. Remove from the heat and stir in the egg yolks. Warm through, stirring all the time. Do not allow it to boil or the egg yolks will curdle. Add the mushrooms. Serve with roast goose, duck or game.

MUSTARD SAUCE

3 egg yolks
1 dessertspoon sugar
2 tablespoons olive oil
2 tablespoons wine vinegar
1 tablespoon either capers or chopped olives
1 small teaspoon made English mustard

Put the yolks, sugar and mustard into a bowl and mix thoroughly with wooden spoon. Add the olive oil gradually beating all the time until it is all used up and the mixture thickens. Dilute with the vinegar and add the capers or chopped olives. The capers give a sharper flavour. This sauce is excellent with cold salmon or halibut, fish pâté (p. 18), grilled herrings or mackerel. If the capers or olives are omitted it can be used as a dressing for Russian salad (p. 98).

HORSERADISH WITH SOUR CREAM

1 horseradish root
1–2 tablespoons vinegar
¼ pt sour cream
1 teaspoon sugar
salt

Grate the horseradish and pour the mixture of vinegar, sour cream, sugar and salt over it. Serve with studen and fish pâté.

MAYONNAISE

1 egg yolk
1 teaspoon sugar
pinch of salt, pepper
1 teaspoon English made mustard

Up to ¼ pt olive oil
1 tablespoon wine vinegar or lemon juice

Mix the egg yolk with the sugar, salt, pepper and mustard. Add the olive oil drop by drop, stirring all the time. Use up to ¼ pt with each yolk. The mixture should be very thick before you add the vinegar or lemon juice. Keep in the fridge in an airtight jar.

MAYONNAISE WITH SOUR CREAM

¼ pt mayonnaise (see above)
¼ pt sour cream
1 sprig parsley

1 tablespoon wine vinegar or lemon juice

Mix the mayonnaise with the sour cream and vinegar or lemon juice. Add the finely chopped parsley. This sauce can be used wherever ordinary mayonnaise is used.

SOUR CREAM SAUCE for Salads

4 tablespoons sour cream
1 tablespoon lemon juice or wine vinegar

pinch of salt
½ teaspoon sugar (optional)

Mix the above ingredients in a large cup and use immediately as it will not keep.

FRENCH DRESSING

8 tablespoons olive oil
4 tablespoons wine vinegar or lemon juice

salt, pepper
1 clove garlic (optional)

Peel the clove of garlic and crush it in a basin with the salt. Add the other ingredients and mix well. Use immediately or store in a bottle in the fridge.

EGG AND CAPER DRESSING

2 hard-boiled eggs
½ tablespoon English made mustard
½ teaspoon sugar
salt

2 tablespoons olive oil
¾ tablespoon wine vinegar or lemon juice
1 tablespoon capers

Sieve the egg yolks and beat them with the mustard until they are white. Add the sugar and salt and stir in the oil gradually. Add the vinegar or lemon juice and mix thoroughly. Finally, add the chopped egg-whites and the capers. Serve with cold fish.

MORELLO CHERRY SAUCE

1 lb. morello cherries
1 pt water
sugar to taste
1 tablespoon potato flour or cornflour

1 wineglass port or madeira (optional)
clove (optional)
cinnamon (optional)

Wash, stalk and stone the cherries and stew them in the water and sugar for about 10 minutes or until cooked. Stir in the potato flour mixed with a little water to thicken the juice. If the port or madeira is added a little more potato flour will be needed. Heat the sauce through again. Cinnamon and clove will give a spicy taste. Serve with veal, poultry and game, and with cherry charlotte (p. 152).

RUM SAUCE

½ oz. butter
1 tablespoon flour
¾ pt water

¼ lb. sugar
3 tablespoons white wine
3 tablespoons rum

Make a roux from the butter and flour. Gradually add the water, stirring all the time to obtain a smooth consistency. Boil gently for a few minutes. Add the sugar, wine and rum and bring back to the boil, still stirring.

Serve with rice pudding or the soufflé with wine or rum (p. 154).

APPLE SAUCE OR PURÉE

1½ lb. cooking apples
3 oz. sugar

1 tablespoon water

Peel and core the apples and cut them into slices. Put them in a saucepan with the sugar and water. Cover and cook slowly for 10–20 minutes until tender. Stir from time to time. Sieve.

This quantity makes about 1 pt sauce or purée.

Serve with roast goose or use for making pastila (see p. 140).

Eggs

BREAKFAST EGGS
(serves 6)

2 rusks
1½ oz. butter
6 eggs

salt, pepper
1 spring onion or sprig parsley

Crush the rusks into fine crumbs with a rolling-pin. Brush the bottom and sides of a frying-pan with melted butter and dust with the crumbs. Break the eggs into the pan. Salt and pepper each egg separately. Sprinkle with finely chopped spring onion or parsley and put a knob of butter on each egg. Fry quickly until set. Serve from the pan.

BREAKFAST EGGS WITH MUSHROOMS
(serves 4)

4 oz. mushrooms
bacon fat
1 slice black bread
2 oz. Polish sausage

2 oz. ham
2 tomatoes
4 eggs
salt, pepper

Wash and slice the mushrooms and fry them in bacon fat for about ten minutes until tender. Discard the crust and cut the bread in cubes. Skin the sausage, cut it in slices and divide each slice in four. Chop the ham and cut the tomatoes in half. Add the bread, sausage, ham and tomatoes to the mushrooms and fry for a few minutes. Break four eggs into the pan. Salt and pepper each egg and cook till set. Serve from the pan.

EGGS WITH BLACK BREAD

(serves 6)

¼ lb. ham	6 eggs
2 spring onions	salt, pepper
1 slice black bread	1 oz. butter

Chop the ham and the spring onions finely. Discard the crusts and cut the bread into cubes. Beat the eggs and season. Melt the butter in a thick frying-pan. Fry the ham, onions and bread lightly. Pour in the eggs and cook till firm.

EGGS IN CREAM

(serves 4)

¼ pt sour cream	4 eggs
4 slices French bread	salt, pepper
1 oz. butter	parsley or dill for garnish

Grease a fireproof dish and pour in half the cream. The slices of French bread should be about an inch thick. Discard the soft part of the bread and fry the crusts lightly in butter. Place them in the dish. Beat the eggs, season and pour into the crusts. Alternatively, break a whole egg into each crust and sprinkle with salt and pepper. Cover with the rest of the sour cream and bake in a moderate oven (350°F, Mark 4) till set. Garnish with parsley or dill.

EGGS WITH COURGETTES OR MARROW

(serves 4)

½ lb. courgettes or 8 slices marrow	4 rashers bacon
oil for frying	4 eggs
4 tomatoes	salt, pepper

Top-and-tail courgettes, and slice thinly, or peel marrow, remove seeds, slice and cut each slice in half. Brown on both sides in a little oil. Add the peeled and chopped tomatoes and the bacon and cook for a few minutes. Add the eggs. Salt and pepper well and cook until set.

Pastry

YEAST PASTRY

½ oz. fresh yeast

1 tablespoon sugar

½ pt milk

1 lb. 5 oz. plain flour (approx.)

pinch of salt

2 oz. butter

3 eggs

Cream the yeast and the sugar with a little warm water. Gradually add the warm milk and about half the sifted flour. Beat well with a wooden spoon until the consistency resembles a rather thick pancake batter. Cover with a cloth and leave in a warm place to rise for about half an hour. When the dough has risen to double its original quantity and is full of bubbles add the salt, melted butter, beaten eggs and the rest of the flour. Knead by hand for about half an hour until the dough comes away from the bowl without sticking. The mixture should be firm enough to roll out. Cover with a cloth and leave to rise a second time in a warm place. This may take anything from 1–4 hours depending on the room temperature. When it has doubled in bulk again remove from the bowl and knead lightly on a floured board.

To make pirog (pie): Roll the pastry out about ⅛-inch thick and line a greased baking-tin with half of it. Spread the filling evenly and cover with the rest of the pastry. Pinch the edges and prick with a fork. Leave to rise again for a further half-hour before putting into the oven. Brush with beaten egg if you wish and bake in a fairly hot oven (400°F, Mark 6) for about 20 minutes until golden brown. When ready transfer to a suitable dish, brush with melted butter and cover with a tea-cloth to prevent the crust from hardening.

To make piroshki (small pies) : The quantity of pastry given above will make about 15 piroshki but will only need a third as much filling as the larger pirog. Form the pastry into a roll about 2 inches in diameter and cut off one-inch pieces. Press each piece in the middle to form a small circle and put into each one a heaped teaspoonful of filling. Pinch the edges together over the filling and put the piroshki on a greased baking-sheet. Leave them for about half an hour to rise again. Brush with beaten egg, if you wish, and bake in a fairly hot oven (400°F, Mark 6) for 10–20 minutes until golden brown. Transfer to a suitable dish when ready, brush with melted butter and cover with a tea-cloth.

Piroshki made with yeast pastry can also be fried in deep oil. They should be lifted out with a perforated spoon when they turn golden.

Pirog and piroshki may be eaten hot or cold. If hot, they are always served with butter. They may be served with soup or eaten as a separate course. Pirog and piroshki made from meat, cabbage or mushroom may be eaten with beef or chicken bouillon. Meat pirog makes a specially good accompaniment for shchi. All types of pirog are served with borshch, the only exception being cabbage pirog which is never served with Ukrainian borshch.

SHORT PASTRY

1 lb. self-raising flour	pinch of salt
8 oz. butter	water to mix

Sift the flour into a basin and add a pinch of salt. Cut the butter into small cubes and rub them into the flour with the tips of the fingers until the mixture resembles fine bread-crumbs. Add only enough water to make a stiff dough. Mix with a knife. Roll out very lightly on a floured board. When used for pirog bake in a fairly hot oven (400°F, Mark 6) for about 20 minutes until golden brown.

PUFF PASTRY

12 oz. plain flour
pinch of salt
12 oz. unsalted butter

juice of ½ lemon
cold water to mix

Sift the flour into a basin and add the salt and lemon juice. Rub in an ounce of the butter. Add enough cold water to mix to a soft dough. Knead on a floured board until smooth. Roll out into a square. Form the butter into an oblong and place it on one half of the pastry. Fold over the other half and seal the edges. Roll out slightly. Fold in three and put aside in a cold place for 20 minutes. Repeat this process five or six times being careful not to press out the air bubbles which form.

When ready it can be rolled out to the required thickness and made into a pirog. Put the pirog into the fridge for about 20 minutes and then transfer it immediately to a very hot oven (475°F, Mark 9) and bake for about 20 minutes or until brown.

SOUR CREAM PASTRY

1 lb. self-raising flour
¼ lb. butter
½ pt sour cream

½ teaspoon salt
1 tablespoon sugar
2 eggs

Cut the butter into small cubes. Sift the flour into a basin. Make a well in the centre and add the butter, sour cream, salt, sugar and eggs. Mix the ingredients very thoroughly with a wooden fork. Turn out on to a floured board and knead quickly by hand until the dough is of a smooth, stiff consistency. Leave in a cold place for about 40 minutes.

Roll out and use for pirog or piroshki. Brush with beaten egg and bake in a fairly hot oven (400–450°F, Mark 6–8) for about 20 minutes until brown.

This pastry is especially recommended for mushroom pirog.

PLAIN PASTRY (for Lamb Pirog)

4 tablespoons oil	1 lb. plain flour
water	½ teaspoon salt

Add enough water to the oil to make up half a pint of liquid. Sift the flour into a basin and add the salt. Add the liquid gradually, stirring all the time with a wooden spoon. When it is fairly stiff turn out on to a floured board and knead by hand until it is a smooth, firm consistency. Roll out fairly thinly and make into a pirog. Bake in a hot oven (450°F, Mark 8) for about 25 minutes until brown.

Fillings for pirog and piroshki

The quantities of pastry given in each of the above recipes are sufficient to make a large pirog or about 15 small piroshki. The quantities of fillings given below are also sufficient for a large pirog. Piroshki made from the stated amounts of pastry, only need about a third as much of the filling as a pirog.

RICE AND MUSHROOM PIROG

(serves 4–5)

6 oz. rice	6 oz. mushrooms
salt and pepper	butter for frying
1 large onion	

Boil the rice in salted water until cooked. Strain. Meanwhile, peel and chop the onion and clean the mushrooms. Fry the onion and mushrooms lightly in butter for about 20 minutes. Mix the cooked rice with the onions and mushrooms and season. Cool and use for the pirog.

RICE AND EGG PIROG

(serves 4–5)

6 oz. rice	1–2 oz. butter
salt and pepper	2 hard-boiled eggs

Boil the rice in salted water until cooked. Strain and rinse in cold water. Return to the saucepan and add the butter. Cook over a low heat until it has melted. Stir lightly, season and add the chopped hard-boiled eggs. The ingredients should be well mixed but too much stirring will spoil the rice. Cool and fill the pirog with the mixture.

BEEF PIROG

(serves 4–5)

1 lb. fresh minced beef or beef boiled for stock	butter for frying
	salt and pepper
1 onion	2 hard-boiled eggs

Peel and chop the onion and fry it lightly in butter. If fresh mince is used add it to the onion and fry for about 20 minutes until brown. If the meat has already been cooked put it through a mincer and mix with the fried onion. Season. Add 2–3 tablespoons water or bouillon and the chopped hard-boiled eggs. Make into the pirog.

SALMON PIROG WITH RICE AND EGG

(serves 4–5)

6 oz. rice	2 hard-boiled eggs
salt	1 sprig parsley
2 oz. butter	1½ lb. salmon

Boil the rice in salted water until it is cooked. Strain, rinse in cold water and return to the saucepan. Add an ounce of butter and stir over a low heat until it has melted. Add the chopped hard-boiled eggs and chopped parsley and mix well. Cool. Line a greased tin with the pastry. Spread half the rice mixture over the pastry. Clean and bone the salmon and put small pieces of the fish on top of the rice. Season and dot with butter. Cover with the rest of the rice mixture and the pastry.

For a more economical dish substitute halibut for salmon.

CABBAGE AND EGG PIROG

(serves 4–5)

1 medium white Dutch cabbage	salt and pepper
2 oz. butter	2 hard-boiled eggs
1 onion	

Discard the outer leaves and the thick veins. Wash and drain the cabbage and shred it finely. Melt the butter and fry the chopped onion lightly. Add the cabbage gradually and cook on a low heat, stirring frequently to prevent burning. The cabbage may turn slightly golden, but it should not be allowed to brown. It will take about 45 minutes to cook. Add salt and pepper about 15 minutes before it is ready. Cool. Chop the hard-boiled eggs and mix with the cabbage. Fill the pie with this mixture.

LIVER AND BUCKWHEAT PIROG

(serves 8)

¾ lb. liver (lamb's, pig's or calf's)	1 onion
6 oz. kasha	salt and pepper
2–3 oz. butter	2 hard-boiled eggs

Cook the kasha (see p. 78). Meanwhile, prepare the liver. Remove any skin or membrane and wash in cold water. Cut into small pieces and fry in butter. Peel and chop the onion and cook slowly with the liver for about 10–15 minutes. When ready, chop the liver finely and season. Mix the cooked kasha and the chopped hard-boiled eggs with the liver and onion, adding a little more butter if it is dry. Cool and make into a pirog.

CAUCASIAN LAMB PIROG

(serves 6)

1½ lb. fillet of lamb	1 clove garlic
1 onion	salt and black pepper

Use the plain pastry recipe (see p. 120) for this pirog. Chop the lamb with a sharp knife into very small pieces. Mix with the finely chopped onion and crushed garlic. Add salt and plenty of pepper. It should be highly seasoned. Fill the pie with the mixture. It should be juicy when cooked.

Kouliabaka

Kouliabaka is a rich type of pirog. It has more filling than the ordinary pirog and is made either with puff pastry (see p. 119) or a rich yeast pastry. The ordinary yeast pastry in this book (see p. 117) can be adapted by adding 2 oz. extra butter and a little more flour. The pastry should be rolled out

thicker than for a pirog as there is more weight in the filling.
The actual pie will be smaller, but thicker. Kouliabaka can be
made in the same shape as a pirog or in the shape of a thick,
fat sausage. The same stuffings can be used as for an ordinary
pirog. If it is made from fish, two or more varieties are
usually used and one of these would be a more expensive
type of fish such as salmon or sturgeon.

Kouliabaki are served on special occasions.

FISH KOULIABAKA

(serves 6–8)

PUFF PASTRY (see p. 109)

FILLING

½ lb. white fish or bream	1 sprig parsley or dill
½ lb. halibut	1⅛ pts water
½ lb. salmon	6 oz. coarse grained semolina
1 onion	salt, pepper
1 oz. butter	1 egg

Prepare the pastry in the quantity given (see p. 119). Remove the skin and bones and wash the fish. Peel and chop the
onion finely and fry it lightly in butter with the chopped
parsley or dill. Add to the white fish or bream and chop the
fish with the onion as finely as possible. Meanwhile, bring
the water to the boil and add the salt and semolina. Stir
quickly to prevent lumps from forming. Remove from the
heat when cooked and fold in the beaten egg. Return to the
heat and warm through, stirring all the time. Make sure that
it does not boil. Remove from the heat and add the chopped
white fish, onion and parsley. Adjust the seasoning and leave
to cool.

Roll out the pastry. It should be slightly thicker than for
an ordinary pirog as there is more filling. Line a baking-tin

with half the pastry and spread half the semolina filling over the bottom. Slice the raw halibut and salmon and put the slices on top of the semolina. Season and put in with rest of the semolina and fish mixture. Cover with the rest of the pastry. Trim and pinch the edges and prick with a fork. Brush with beaten egg, if you wish, and put in a hot oven (450–500°F, Mark 8–9) turning down to 400°F, Mark 6 when it starts to brown. Bake for 35–45 minutes.

SPRAT SHANGI

(serves 4–5)

yeast pastry (see p. 117)	butter
1½ lb. fresh sprats	salt

Make the yeast pastry as for a pirog. Wash the fish, top-and-tail them and salt them. Roll out the dough on a floured board and cut into 6-inch squares. Place three fishes top-to-tail on each tart and turn up the edges. Put the shangi on greased baking-sheets and leave in a warm place to rise for another half an hour. Place in a fairly hot oven (400°F, Mark 6) for about 20 minutes. Add a knob of butter to each shangi before serving. This is a dish from Archangel.

PASTE FOR PELMENI AND VARENIKI

½ lb. plain flour	2–3 tablespoons water
salt	1 egg

Sift the flour into a basin. Add the salt. Make a well in the centre and break in the egg. Mix to a fairly stiff paste with a fork, adding a little water at a time. Knead on a floured board until it is smooth and all the flour is worked in. Roll out thinly and use for pelmeni or vareniki. This is the correct amount of paste for the fillings given in the following recipes.

SIBERIAN PELMENI

(serves 4)

PASTE

FILLING

¾ lb. top rump	1 tablespoon finely chopped onion
salt and pepper	(optional)
2 tablespoons water	

Make the paste as in the previous recipe.

Mince the meat very finely. Season and add the onion and water. Mix well. Cut the thinly rolled paste into small rounds with a wineglass and put a teaspoonful of the filling on to each round. Pinch the edges together to make small 'pies'. Use a little water if the pastry will not stick. Drop the pelmeni into boiling salted water, bone stock or bouillon (see pp. 21–2), and simmer for 10–15 minutes. Serve in the liquid or lift out and transfer to a dish with melted butter and serve with sour cream or vinegar and mustard.

Eat as a main course.

VARENIKI WITH CURD CHEESE

(serves 4)

PASTE

FILLING

¾ lb. curd cheese	1 oz. butter
1 egg	salt
1½ oz. sugar	⅓ pt sour cream

Make the paste (see p. 125). Sieve the cheese to remove any lumps. Add the egg yolk, sugar and ½ oz. melted butter. Home-made cheese (see p. 175) may need a little salt, but bought cheese is usually salty enough. Mix thoroughly with a wooden spoon. Cut the thinly rolled paste into small rounds with a wine or sherry glass. Put a teaspoonful of the mixture on to each round. Dab the edges with beaten egg-white and pinch them together to form small 'pies'. Drop the vareniki into boiling salted water and simmer for 10–15 minutes until they rise to the surface. Lift them out with a perforated spoon. Melt the remaining butter and pour into a warm dish. Put in the vareniki and serve with sour cream.

Eat as a main course.

VARENIKI WITH DAMSONS OR CHERRIES

(serves 6)

PASTE

FILLING

¾ lb. morello cherries or damsons	pinch of salt
3–4 oz. sugar	½ pt sour cream
⅓ pt water	castor sugar

Make the paste (see p. 125). Stone the cherries or damsons and cover them with the sugar. Leave for several hours in the sun, if possible, to absorb the sugar. Remove the kernels from a few of the stones and crush them. Boil them in ⅓ pt water for a few minutes and strain. When the fruit is ready add any of the juice which has formed and any of the sugar which has not been absorbed and boil for a few minutes to make a syrup.

Cut the thinly rolled paste into rounds. Put either 1 damson or 2 cherries on each round and pinch the edges firmly together. Drop them into boiling salted water and simmer until they float to the top. Lift out with a perforated spoon and drain off all the water. Transfer to a warm dish and pour over the hot syrup. Serve with sour cream and castor sugar.

MOSCOW PASTRY

½ lb. butter	1 lb. self-raising flour
¼ lb. vanilla sugar	rind of 1 lemon
1 egg	

Cream the butter and vanilla sugar until white. Add the beaten egg and grated lemon rind. Beat. Gradually fold in the sifted flour and mix with the hands to a firm dough. It will not be as stiff as English short-pastry and is more difficult to handle but it is worth the extra trouble. Use for vatrushka (see p. 129) and all tarts. Bake in a fairly hot oven (400°F, Mark 6) for 20 minutes until golden brown.

SWEET YEAST PASTRY

½ oz. yeast	3 oz. butter
1 teaspoon sugar	2 eggs and 1 yolk
1¼ lb. plain flour	3 oz. vanilla sugar
½ pt milk	pinch of salt

Cream the yeast with a teaspoon of sugar and a little warm water. Warm the milk and add it to the yeast mixture together with half the sifted flour. Beat well to make a batter. Cover with a cloth and leave in a warm place to rise for about half an hour. When it has doubled its original size and there are bubbles on top add the melted butter, eggs, vanilla sugar, salt and the rest of the sifted flour. Knead well for about half an hour until the dough comes away from the sides of the bowl without sticking. Cover with a cloth and leave to rise a second time in a warm place. When it has doubled its bulk again knead lightly on a floured board and roll out. Make into a tart and leave to rise a third time for half an hour before putting in the oven. Bake in a fairly hot oven (400°F, Mark 6) for about 20 minutes. Use for making vatrushka (see p. 129) and all tarts.

VATRUSHKA

(serves 4–6)

Moscow or sweet yeast pastry (see
p. 128).

rind of 1 lemon
a few sultanas (optional)
2 eggs
2 tablespoons fresh cream

FILLING
1½ lb. curb cheese
6 oz. vanilla sugar

Make Moscow or sweet yeast pastry in the quantities given.
FILLING: Sieve the cheese to remove any lumps and add the
vanilla sugar. The amount of cheese used can be varied and
the amount of sugar needed depends on whether the cheese
is home-made or bought. Bought cheese usually needs more
sugar. Add the grated lemon rind, sultanas, beaten eggs and
cream and mix well.

Roll out the pastry and line a large tin. Spread the cheese
mixture evenly and turn up the edges of the tart. Strips of
pastry can be laid across the tart. Brush the pastry with
beaten egg if you wish. If sweet yeast pastry has been used
leave the pastry to rise for half an hour before putting it in
the oven. Bake in a fairly hot oven (400°F, Mark 6) for
about 20 minutes. Moscow pastry should also be cooked for
about 20 minutes but will need a slightly hotter oven
425°F, Mark 6–7).

Blini

Blini are pancakes made with yeast. They are served very
hot with plenty of melted butter, sour cream and a large
selection of salted fish and caviar. Although in Russia they
are served as an extra dish they are sufficiently filling to be
served as a main course. It is a good idea to start the meal
with bouillon as this helps to counteract the salty effects of
the fish. Blini are traditionally eaten in the week before Lent.

To serve put 2 or 3 blini at a time on warm plates and pour over as much melted butter and sour cream as required. The blini should be folded over or rolled and eaten with one of the varieties of salted fish or caviar.

BLINI
(serves 8)

1 lb. 9 oz. plain flour	1 teaspoon salt
2 oz. yeast	1 oz. sugar
1¼ pts warm water	1 pt milk
2 oz. melted butter	butter or oil for frying
3 eggs	

Mix the yeast with a little warm water to a smooth paste. Add the rest of the warm water and half the sifted flour. Mix with a wooden spoon, cover and leave in a warm place for about half an hour. It should rise to approximately double its original quantity and be full of bubbles. Gradually add the rest of the sifted flour, beating until the mixture is smooth. Stir in the melted butter, egg yolks, sugar and salt. Warm the milk and add it gradually until a smooth batter is obtained. Leave in a warm place to rise a second time. Beat the egg whites until they stand in peaks and fold them in when the mixture has doubled. Allow it to rise a third time. The batter should be full of bubbles. Heat two small frying-pans with thick bases and brush them with melted butter or oil. Pour tablespoons of the batter into the frying-pans. The blini should be very thin when cooked and full of holes like lace. The first blini are often rather thick and can be discarded. If the batter seems too thick a little more warm milk can be added carefully. Keep the first blini in a warm dish while you are frying the others. The rest of the batter can be left for a short time while you are eating the first batch. These quantities should make about 32 blini.

Blini can also be made from a mixture of buckwheat and plain white flour. The method and other ingredients are exactly the same. Add 1 lb. of sifted buckwheat flour in the first stage and 9 oz. of sifted white flour in the second. A little more salt can be used.

BASIC PANCAKES

(10 pancakes)

¼ lb. self-raising flour	1 egg
pinch of salt	½ pt milk
1 teaspoon sugar	butter or oil for frying

Sift the flour and salt into a basin with the sugar. Add the egg. Beat with a wooden spoon, gradually adding the milk. Leave for half an hour. Heat a frying-pan, brush with oil or melted butter and pour in about two tablespoons of batter, tilting the pan so that it is evenly covered. Fry on one side until brown. Turn or toss carefully and fry on the other side. Put aside to keep warm while the other pancakes are cooking. If the first pancake is too thick dilute the batter with a little warm milk. Serve with jam or lemon juice and castor sugar.

This pancake mixture is suitable for making blinchati piroshki (see below) or quick pancakes with cream cheese (see p. 132).

BLINCHATI PIROSHKI

(10 pancakes)

basic pancake batter (see above)	1 small onion
butter	butter for frying
dry breadcrumbs	salt and pepper
	1 hard-boiled egg
FILLING	1 sprig dill or parsley
½ lb. minced meat (beef, veal or pork)	

Make the basic pancake batter in the quantities given on p. 131.

FILLING: Fry the peeled and chopped onion lightly in butter. If fresh mince is used add it to the onion and fry for about 20 minutes until brown. If the meat is already cooked put it through the mincer and add the fried onion. Add a little water too or the stuffing will be too dry. Season and add the chopped hard-boiled egg and chopped dill or parsley. Heat through. The filling should be ready at the same time as the pancakes.

Cook the pancakes but leave one side fairly white. Put a tablespoon of the filling on to the brown side. Turn the edges over to form a small 'envelope', sprinkle with dry breadcrumbs, dot with butter and brown for a few minutes under the grill. Serve with bouillon.

QUICK PANCAKES WITH CREAM CHEESE

(10 pancakes)

basic pancake batter (see p. 131)
¼ pt sour cream
sugar

1 small egg
1 oz. vanilla sugar
a few sultanas (optional)

FILLING
½ lb. curd cheese

FILLING: Sieve the cheese to remove any lumps. Add the beaten egg, vanilla sugar and sultanas and mix well.

Make the pancakes. When they are all cooked put a tablespoon of the filling on to each pancake and roll up. Brown on both sides for a few minutes under the grill. Sprinkle with sugar and serve with sour cream.

CREAM PANCAKES

(8 pancakes)

2 large eggs	1 tablespoon milk
1 tablespoon sugar	1 carton single cream (3.25 fl. oz.)
2 oz. butter	butter or oil for frying
¼ lb. self-raising flour	

Beat the eggs and sugar well with a fork. Melt the butter and beat it into the mixture. Sift the flour into another basin and mix with the milk and cream. Gradually add the mixture of eggs, sugar and butter to the flour, beating all the time until it is smooth. Leave for 1–2 hours. Heat a frying-pan with a thick base and brush with oil or butter. Pour in about two tablespoons of batter and fry on one side until brown. Turn or toss carefully and fry on the other side. If the first pancake is too thick, dilute the batter with a little warm milk. Serve with jam or castor sugar and lemon juice.

Cakes

PRYANIK (Honey Cake)

2 eggs
2 oz. sugar
⅛ pt vegetable oil
2 tablespoons honey

pinch of baking powder
6 oz. self-raising flour
½ teaspoon powdered cinnamon

Beat the egg yolks with the sugar. Warm the oil and honey a little and add to the egg yolks. Mix in the flour, baking powder and cinnamon. Beat the egg-whites until they stand in peaks and fold them into the mixture. Transfer to a greased baking-tin and bake in a moderate oven (350°F, Mark 4) for about 40 minutes.

PRYANIKI

15 oz. self-raising flour
½ teaspoon powdered cloves
½ teaspoon powdered nutmeg
½ teaspoon powdered cinnamon
½ teaspoon powdered ginger
¼ teaspoon powdered cardamom
¼ teaspoon baking powder

2 eggs
8 oz. brown sugar

GLAZE
¼ pt water
12 oz. sugar
2 egg-whites

Sift the flour, baking powder and spices into a bowl. Beat the eggs and sugar for about five minutes and add them to the flour mixture. Mix well. The dough should be stiff and fairly sticky. Roll into balls of about 1-inch in diameter. Put on a greased baking-sheet and bake in a moderate oven (375°F, Mark 5) for about 15 minutes.

GLAZE: Meanwhile, boil the water and sugar to form a

syrup. Beat the egg-whites until stiff and pour the syrup into the egg-whites. Beat well. Dip the pryaniki in the glaze while they are still hot. Cool on a wire tray.

This quantity will make about 3½ dozen pryaniki.

VANILLA, LEMON OR PEPPERMINT PRYANIKI

½ lb. castor sugar   6 oz. sifted flour
2 large eggs

BASIC METHOD: Beat the eggs with the sugar until white. Gradually fold in the sifted flour. Butter three baking-trays. Put teaspoonfuls of the mixture on the trays and bake in a fairly hot oven (400°F, Mark 6).

For vanilla pryaniki: Use vanilla sugar instead of ordinary sugar.

For lemon pryaniki: Add the grated rind of one lemon to the above mixture.

For peppermint pryaniki: Add two saltspoonfuls of oil of peppermint to the mixture.

This recipe will make about 36 pryaniki.

KHVOROST

1 egg   ½ teaspoon salt
1 oz. sugar   ½ lb. plain flour
¼ pt milk   butter and/or oil for frying
1 sherry glass rum   icing sugar

Beat the egg with the sugar until white. Stir in the milk, rum and salt. Sift in the flour and mix well to a stiff paste. Knead on a floured board until smooth. Roll out thinly and cut into strips of about 4 inches by 1 inch. Make a slit down the middle and thread one end through the slit (see diagram). Deep fry in oil or butter or a mixture of the two until

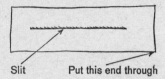

Slit   Put this end through

Should look like this

golden brown. Remove with a perforated spoon and drain on greaseproof paper. Dredge with sifted icing sugar before serving and eat on the same day.

MOSCOW DOUGHNUTS

½ oz. yeast	pinch of salt
1 oz. sugar	pinch grated nutmeg, cinnamon or
¼ pt milk	cardamom
10 oz. plain flour	jam for filling
2 egg yolks	oil or butter for frying
2 oz. butter	icing or castor sugar for coating

Mix the yeast with a teaspoonful of sugar and a little water to a smooth paste. Add the warm milk and about half the sifted flour. Cover with a cloth and leave to rise in a warm place for about half an hour until it has doubled its bulk and is full of bubbles. Gradually add the yolks and sugar, beating all the time. Melt the butter and allow it to cool slightly. Add the butter to the yeast mixture together with the rest of the sifted flour, salt and spice. Knead for about half an hour until the dough leaves the sides of the bowl without sticking. Cover and leave to rise a second time. When it has doubled its bulk again roll out on a floured board to about ½-inch thick. Cut in rounds with a glass. Put a teaspoonful of jam on each round and fold up the edges to form a ball. Leave for another half an hour to rise. Deep fry in very hot oil or butter until brown. Drain on greaseproof paper. Coat in icing or castor sugar before serving.

KRENDEL (Birthday Cake)

1½ oz. yeast	6 oz. vanilla sugar
1 teaspoon sugar	pinch of salt
⅜ pt milk	3 oz. sultanas
1 lb. 1 oz. plain flour	2 tablespoons icing sugar
6 egg yolks	2 oz. blanched almonds
5 oz. butter	

Mix the yeast with a teaspoonful of sugar and a little warm water to a smooth paste. Add the warm milk and half the sifted flour. Beat well. Cover with a cloth and leave in a warm place to rise until it has doubled its bulk and has bubbles on top. Add the yolks and the vanilla sugar, stirring all the time. Melt the butter and allow it to cool slightly. Add gradually to the yeast mixture together with the salt, sultanas and remaining flour. Knead well by hand for about half an hour until the dough leaves the sides of the bowl without sticking. Cover with a cloth and leave in a warm place until it has again doubled in bulk. Knead lightly on a floured board. Roll out into a long sausage shape with tapering ends. Make a figure-of-eight by looping the two ends round to the middle of the sausage. Leave on a greased baking-sheet for a further half an hour to rise again. Brush the top of the krendel with beaten egg and sprinkle with chopped almonds. Bake in a moderate oven (350°F, Mark 4) for 40–50 minutes. When cool, sprinkle with sifted icing sugar.

SOUR CREAM RUSKS

2 eggs	¼ pt sour cream
4 oz. sugar	12 oz. self-raising flour
2 oz. butter	

Beat the eggs with the sugar until they are white. Beat the butter until it is soft and add it to the eggs and sugar. Fold in the sour cream. Add the sifted flour gradually until the mixture is stiff enough to roll out. Roll out on a floured board making long sausage shapes about 2 inches in diameter. Bake in a moderate oven (375°F, Mark 5) for about 15–20 minutes until brown. Cool on a wooden board and cut in slices ¾-inch thick. Put on baking-sheets and dry in a slow oven (200°F, Mark ¼) for 1–2 hours. Store in an airtight tin.

VANILLA RUSKS

1 oz. yeast	6 oz. butter
¼ pt plus 2 tablespoons milk	6 oz. sugar
1 lb. 9 oz. flour	vanilla essence
pinch of salt	grated nutmeg (optional)
4 eggs	

Mix the yeast with a teaspoon of sugar in a little warm water to a smooth paste. Gradually add the warm milk and about half the sifted flour. Beat well with a wooden spoon until it resembles a thick pancake batter. Cover with a cloth and leave in a warm place to rise for about half an hour until it has doubled its original bulk and is full of bubbles. Mix together the eggs and sugar and melt the butter and allow it to cool slightly. Add these together with the rest of the sifted flour, salt, vanilla essence and nutmeg. Knead by hand for about half an hour until the dough comes away from the sides of the bowl. Cover with a cloth and leave in a warm place to rise a second time. When it has doubled its bulk again turn it out on to a floured board. Butter two meat-tins and form the dough into four sausages the length of the tins. Leave them to rise a third time in the tins. Bake in a moderate oven (350°F, Mark 4) for about 20 minutes until well browned and risen. Cool on a wooden board. The following day cut into slices about ¼-inch thick and put on baking-sheets to dry for 2–3 hours in a slow oven (200°F, Mark ¼). When ready the rusks will be golden and dry all the way through. Store in airtight tins.

PASTILA

½ pt apple purée (see p. 111)   ¼ lb. sugar
1 egg-white

Make the apple purée. Beat the egg-white until it stands in peaks and fold it into the purée with the sugar. Spread about ½-inch thick on a greased baking-sheet and dry in a very slow oven (200°F, Mark ¼) for 3–4 hours. Cut into squares. Serve with Russian tea.

MERINGUES

3 egg-whites   3 oz. granulated sugar
pinch of salt   3 oz. castor sugar

Chill the egg-whites and beat them with a pinch of salt until they stand in peaks. Gently add half the sugar and continue beating until the mixture is very thick. Fold in the rest of the sugar. Put teaspoonfuls on a greased baking-sheet and bake for 2–3 hours in a very slow oven (200°F, Mark ¼). Store in an airtight tin.

RUM BABAS

½ oz. yeast   1 oz. currants (optional)
1 oz. sugar
¼ pt milk   SAUCE
9 oz. plain flour   1 pt water
¼ lb. butter   6 oz. castor sugar
3 eggs   2 wineglasses rum
pinch of salt

Mix the yeast with a teaspoonful of sugar and a little warm water to a smooth paste. Add the warm milk and half the sifted flour. Cover and leave to rise in a warm place for about half an hour until it has doubled its bulk and there are bubbles on top. Add the sugar and eggs, stirring all the time. Melt the butter and cool slightly. Add the butter to the yeast mixture together with the rest of the sifted flour, and the salt and currants. Beat well with a wooden spoon for 5–10 minutes until the dough is smooth and shiny. Cover and leave in a warm place to rise a second time. When it has doubled its bulk again stir lightly to remove air bubbles and transfer to a greased cake-ring or small greased cake-tins. Leave to rise again for half an hour before putting in the oven. Bake in a moderate oven (350°F, Mark 4) for 25–30 minutes for the cake-ring or 15–20 minutes for the small tins.

SAUCE: Dissolve the sugar in boiling water and add the rum. Turn out the baba when cooked and pour the sauce over while it is still hot. Glaze with sieved apricot jam, if you wish. Decorate with whipped cream when cool.

BULKA (Yeast Cake)

1 oz. yeast	6 oz. vanilla sugar
½ pt milk	pinch of salt
1 lb. 6 oz. plain flour	2 tablespoons sultanas
¼ lb. butter	2 tablespoons mixed peel
3 eggs	pinch of nutmeg or cardamom

Mix the yeast with a teaspoonful of sugar and a little warm water to a smooth paste. Add the warm milk and half the sifted flour. Beat well. Cover with a cloth and leave to rise in a warm place for about half an hour until it has doubled its original bulk and is full of bubbles. Melt the butter and add it together with the remainder of the flour and the other ingredients. Knead well by hand for about half an hour until the dough leaves the sides of the bowl. Cover with a cloth and leave to rise in a warm place until it has again doubled its bulk. Line a tin with buttered greaseproof paper. Knead the mixture lightly and transfer it to the tin. Leave for about half an hour to rise again and bake in a moderate oven (350°F, Mark 4) for 1–1¼ hours. Serve with or without butter for breakfast or afternoon tea.

POPPY SEED ROLL

PASTRY	FILLING
nearly 1 oz. yeast	1½ lb. poppy seeds
½ pt milk	½ lb. sugar or honey
1 lb. 5 oz. plain flour (approx.)	1 oz. sultanas
pinch of salt	1 oz. chopped walnuts
4 oz. butter	1 tablespoon icing sugar
4 oz. sugar	
3 eggs	

Cream the yeast with a teaspoon of sugar and a little warm water. Warm the milk and add it to the yeast mixture together with half the sifted flour. Beat well until the consistency resembles a thick batter. Cover with a cloth and leave in a warm place to rise for about half an hour. When it has doubled its original size and there are bubbles on top, add the melted butter, sugar, eggs, salt and the rest of the flour. Knead well by hand until the mixture comes away from the sides of the bowl without sticking. Cover with a cloth and leave to rise for a second time in a warm place. When it has doubled its bulk again knead lightly on a floured board and roll out to about ⅓-inch thick.

FILLING: Meanwhile, cover the poppy seeds with boiling water and leave them to stand for about half an hour. Squeeze out all the liquid. Put the seeds through a mincer two or three times. Blend in the sugar or honey, sultanas and chopped walnuts. Spread the mixture over the pastry and roll up as for a Swiss roll. This quantity will make two rolls. Leave to rise for a further half an hour on a greased baking-tray before putting in the oven. Bake in a moderate oven (350°F, Mark 4) for 20–30 minutes. When ready, cool on a wooden board. Dust with sifted icing sugar.

BREAKFAST BUNS

½ oz. yeast   2 oz. butter
1 tablespoon sugar   2 eggs
¼ pt milk   pinch of salt
½ lb. plain flour

Mix the yeast with a teaspoon of sugar and a little warm water to a smooth paste. Add the warm milk and half the sifted flour and beat well with a wooden spoon. Cover with a cloth and leave in a warm place to rise. When it has doubled its bulk and there are bubbles on top add the melted butter, sugar, eggs, salt and the rest of the flour. Beat with a wooden spoon for 5–10 minutes until thoroughly mixed. Cover with a cloth and leave to rise a second time. When it has doubled its bulk again beat with a wooden spoon and put the mixture into small buttered cake-tins allowing enough room in each tin for the mixture to double its volume. Leave to rise again and then bake in a moderate oven (350°F, Mark 4) for about 20 minutes.

This quantity will make twelve buns.

KULICH (Easter Cake)

1 oz. yeast   ½ lb. vanilla sugar
1 teaspoon sugar   ¼ lb. candied peel
½ pt milk   ¼ lb. sultanas
1 lb. 5 oz. flour (plain)   2 oz. blanched almonds
½ lb. butter   1 or 2 powdered cardamom seeds
3 eggs and 2 yolks   pinch of salt

This quantity makes one large kulich. Mix the yeast with a teaspoonful of sugar and a little warm water to a smooth paste. Add the warm milk and about ½ lb. of sifted flour and beat till the consistency resembles a batter. Cover and leave in a warm place for about half an hour to rise . When it has doubled its bulk and there are bubbles on top, add the melted butter, eggs, vanilla sugar, peel, sultanas, chopped almonds, cardamom, salt and the rest of the sifted flour. Knead well until the dough comes away from the sides of the bowl without sticking. Cover and leave in warm place to rise a second time. Line a deep tin (8 inches deep, 6 inches wide) with buttered greaseproof paper. When the mixture has doubled in bulk again, flatten with the hand and transfer it to the tin. Leave to rise until the dough almost reaches the top of the tin. It will rise again in the oven. Bake on the bottom shelf in a moderate oven (350°F, Mark 4) for one to one and a quarter hours. When ready, turn out and cover with a clean towel. Cool and ice the top with pink or white icing (see p. 146) or sour cream icing (see p. 147). Sprinkle the icing with hundreds and thousands or decorate with confectioner's roses.

Cut in slices about 1¼ inches thick and eat at Easter with Paskha (pp. 167–9).

SPONGE

4 eggs	rind of 1 lemon
vanilla sugar	icing or filling (see pp. 146–7)
flour	

Take the weight of the eggs in vanilla sugar and flour. Beat the eggs for about five minutes. Gradually add the sugar and grated lemon rind, beating all the time. Beat for a further five minutes and fold in the flour. Put into a greased baking-tin (10 inches by 8 inches) and bake on the middle shelf in a moderate oven (375°F, Mark 5) for 40–45 minutes. Cool on a rack. Use any of the fillings or icings in this chapter.

EASTER NUT CAKE

5 large eggs
½ lb. castor sugar
rind of 1 lemon
pinch of salt

few drops lemon juice or 1 teaspoon
  rum
½ lb. shelled hazel nuts

Grate the nuts in their skins. Beat the egg yolks with the sugar until they are white. Add the grated lemon rind and lemon juice or rum. Beat the egg-whites with a pinch of salt until they stand in peaks and fold them into the mixture. Add the grated nuts. Put the mixture in a greased cake-tin in a moderate oven (375°F, Mark 5) for about 40 minutes. It will shrink slightly when cooled. Ice when cool with mocha or chocolate butter icing (p. 147) or use the fresh-whipped cream filling in any flavour (p. 146) either as a filling or a topping.

EASTER ALMOND CAKE

4 egg-whites
pinch of salt
3 oz. sugar
¼ lb. shelled almonds

rind of ½ lemon
1 tablespoon rum or rose water
few drops almond essence

Grate the almonds. Beat the egg-whites with a pinch of salt until they stand in peaks. Add the sugar gradually, beating all the time until the mixture becomes very thick. Fold in the rum or rose water, the grated lemon rind, nuts, and almond essence. Line an 8-inch sandwich-tin with grease-proof paper. Brush with oil and transfer the mixture to the tin. Bake in a moderate oven (375°F, Mark 5) for about 30 minutes. Cool on a wire tray and ice the top with mocha or chocolate butter icing or sour cream icing (p. 147).

COFFEE AND CHOCOLATE NUT CAKE

6 oz. shelled walnuts	½ teaspoon powdered coffee
4 eggs	1 teaspoon cocoa
¼ lb. icing sugar	1 teaspoon dry breadcrumbs

Grate the nuts or chop them very finely. Beat the egg yolks with the sifted icing sugar until white. Add the coffee and cocoa and blend well. Beat the whites until they stand in peaks and fold them into the mixture. Add the grated nuts and breadcrumbs. Grease and line a 9-inch cake-tin and transfer the mixture. Bake for about 30 minutes in a moderate oven (350°F, Mark 4).

Cool on a wire tray and ice the top of the cake with mocha or chocolate butter icing (p. 147), whipped cream topping (p. 146) or sour cream icing (p. 147).

PINK OR WHITE ICING

1 egg-white	1 dessertspoon red wine or 2 teaspoons
½ lb. icing sugar	lemon juice and grated rind ½ lemon

Beat the egg-white until it begins to stiffen. Add the sieved icing sugar gradually, beating all the time. Add the wine for pink icing or the lemon juice and rind for white. Continue beating until the mixture is thick and smooth.

Half this quantity of icing is enough for the top of one kulich (p. 143). The full quantity will very generously cover the sponge (p. 144).

WHIPPED CREAM TOPPING OR FILLING

⅓ pt double cream	2 teaspoons rum
2 teaspoons sugar	1 small egg-white (optional)

Whip the cream until stiff. Fold in the sugar and rum. If

you prefer a lighter consistency, beat an egg-white until it stands in peaks and fold it in to the cream.

COFFEE FLAVOUR: Add 2 teaspoons of strong black coffee to the above mixture.

CHOCOLATE FLAVOUR: Add a few drops of vanilla essence and a teaspoon of cocoa to the above mixture. Mix the cocoa with the sugar and dissolve them in a little warm water.

The above quantities are sufficient to cover or fill a 9-inch cake. This cream will not keep unless it is left in the fridge overnight.

MOCHA ICING

4 oz. unsalted butter
4 oz. icing sugar
1 small egg yolk

a few drops vanilla essence
2 teaspoons strong black coffee

Cream the butter with a wooden spoon until white. Add the egg yolk and continue beating until well blended. Beat in the sifted icing sugar gradually. Add the vanilla essence and coffee and mix thoroughly.

The above quantity will ice or fill the sponge or ice the top of any of the nut cakes.

CHOCOLATE BUTTER ICING

Use the same proportions of ingredients as above, substituting 2 teaspoonfuls of cocoa mixed with a little sugar and warm water for the black coffee. Use for the same cakes.

SOUR CREAM ICING

½ lb. icing sugar
1 teaspoon lemon or orange juice
3 teaspoons sour cream
1 small egg-white

a few drops lemon or orange essence
or grated rind of lemon or small
orange

Sift the icing sugar into a basin. Add the lemon or orange juice, the rind or essence and the sour cream. Beat the egg-white until it stands in peaks and fold it in to the mixture. Beat with a wooden spoon until it is smooth and thick.

This quantity is enough to ice the tops of two 6–8-inch cakes.

Puddings

BERRY KISSEL
(serves 4–6)

1 lb. strawberries or raspberries
1 pt water

4 oz. sugar (approx.)
2 tablespoons potato flour or arrowroot

Stalk and clean the fruit and put it in a saucepan with the water. Bring to the boil, reduce heat and simmer for at least 15 minutes. The softer the fruit the more juice can be extracted. Strain through a fine wire sieve or muslin. Avoid pressing it too much as this makes the kissel cloudy. Return the juice to the saucepan, keeping back a little of the liquid to blend with the flour. Add the sugar to the saucepan and bring to the boil. Add the blended flour and liquid and simmer for a few minutes stirring briskly all the time. Serve hot or cold with castor sugar and cream or milk.

This kissel can also be made with gooseberries, blackcurrants or morello cherries. Adjust the amount of sugar to the type of fruit.

To make a thinner kissel or a fruit sauce use half the amount of flour.

APPLE KISSEL
(serves 4–5)

1 lb. cooking apples
1 pt water
1 slice lemon rind

juice ½ lemon
¼ lb. sugar
1 tablespoon potato flour or arrowroot

Peel, core and slice the apples. Cook them in the water with the lemon rind for about 20 minutes until tender.

Sieve. Add the lemon juice and sugar and return to the saucepan. Bring to the boil. Mix the flour with a little water and stir it into the purée. Cook for a few minutes, stirring all the time until it thickens. Serve hot or cold, with or without cream.

MILK KISSEL

(serves 4)

1 pt milk
1½ oz. sugar
flavouring (optional)

2 level tablespoons potato flour or arrowroot

Put the sugar and most of the milk into a saucepan and bring to the boil. Mix the flour with the remaining milk and add to the boiling kissel, stirring all the time until it thickens. Flavour with vanilla or almond essence or grated lemon or orange rind. Serve with fruit.

KISSEL WITH WINE

(serves 6)

1 lb. berries (cranberries, blackberries, redcurrants, etc.)
1 pt water
4 oz. sugar

¼ pt dry red wine
3 dessertspoons potato flour or arrowroot

Stalk and clean the fruit and put it into a saucepan with the water. Bring to the boil, reduce heat and simmer for about 15 minutes. Put the fruit through a fine wire sieve or muslin. Return the juice to the saucepan, add the sugar and bring to the boil. Mix the wine with the flour and add to the juice. Stir until it thickens. Serve hot or cold with cream and castor sugar. Cold kissel can be decorated with whipped cream and chopped blanched almonds.

COMPÔTE OF FRESH FRUIT

(serves 6)

½ lb. cooking apples	½ lb. apricots
½ lb. morello cherries	1 2 oz. sugar
½ lb. yellow plums	1 pt water

Peel, core and slice the apples. Stalk and wash the other fruit. Stone the cherries very carefully so that the cherries remain whole. Boil the cherry stones in the sugar and water for a few minutes. Strain and add the apples. Simmer gently for about 10 minutes. Add the whole apricots, plums and cherries. Simmer for a further 10 minutes or until the fruit is tender.

FRESH BERRIES WITH SUGAR AND WINE

(serves 6)

1 ½ lb. mixed fruit (blackcurrants, redcurrants, strawberries, raspberries, cherries, gooseberries or grapes)	½ lb. castor sugar
	4 wineglasses sherry, madeira or muscat

Use a mixture of any three fruits available. Stalk and wash the fruit, removing the stones from the cherries and pips from the grapes. Put the fruit into a glass dish. Cover with sugar and pour the wine or sherry over. Leave to stand for 2 or 3 hours before serving.

VOZDUSHNI PIROG (1) (Air Pudding with Apples)

(serves 6)

1 ½ lb. cooking apples	6 egg-whites
6 oz. castor sugar	pinch of salt

Peel and core the apples and cook them with the sugar in a very little water until tender. Sieve to make a purée. Cool. Beat the egg-whites with a pinch of salt until they stand in peaks. Fold the apple purée into the egg-whites and put the mixture into a greased soufflé-dish. Bake in a fairly hot oven (400°F, Mark 6) for about 15 minutes until brown and risen. Serve immediately.

VOZDUSHNI PIROG (2) (Air Pudding with Jam)

(serves 6)

6 egg-whites	2 oz. castor sugar
pinch of salt	¼ pt single cream
4–6 oz. strawberry or raspberry jam	

Beat the whites with a pinch of salt until they stand in peaks. Fold the sugar and jam into the egg-whites. If the jam is stiff, add a little water to it. Pour the mixture into a greased soufflé-dish, sprinkle with sugar and bake in a fairly hot oven (400°F, Mark 6) for about 15 minutes until brown and risen. Serve immediately with single cream.

CHERRY CHARLOTTE

(serves 6)

6 eggs	3 oz. breadcrumbs
6 oz. sugar	4 oz. melted butter
½ pt milk	1 lb. stoned morello cherries
1 teaspoon cinnamon	1 teaspoon mixed peel (optional)

Separate the eggs and beat the yolks with the sugar until white. Add the milk, cinnamon and breadcrumbs. Stir in the melted butter, when it has cooled slightly, and mix well. Add the cherries and the peel. Beat the whites until very stiff and fold them into the mixture. Put the mixture in a greased soufflé-dish which has been dusted with breadcrumbs and bake for about half an hour in a moderate oven (350–400°F, Mark 4–6) until brown and risen. Serve with cherry sauce (p. 110).

APRICOT SOUFFLÉ

(serves 6)

1 lb. apricots
⅓ pt water (approx.)
4 oz. sugar
1 dessertspoon flour

1 oz. butter
4 eggs
1 tablespoon rum or sherry

Wash and stone the apricots and cut them in small pieces. Put them in a saucepan with the water, cover and simmer for about 15 minutes or until tender. Put through a coarse sieve and return to the saucepan. Add the sugar and cook slowly for about five minutes until the mixture turns a deeper colour. Do not let it thicken too much at this stage. Mix the flour to a smooth paste with a tablespoon of water and add it to the purée, stirring all the time until it has heated through. The mixture should thicken further. Stir in the butter and put aside to cool slightly. Separate the eggs and add the beaten egg yolks and the rum or sherry. Beat the egg-whites until they stand in peaks and fold them into the mixture. Transfer the mixture to a greased soufflé-dish, sprinkle with a little castor sugar and bake in a fairly hot oven (400°F, Mark 6) for about 30 minutes or until brown and risen. Serve by itself or with egg custard (p.156).

This soufflé can also be made from morello cherries or damsons. Adjust the amount of sugar to the type of fruit used.

SOUFFLÉ WITH WINE OR RUM

(serves 4–6)

2 oz. butter
2½ oz. white breadcrumbs
¼ pt white wine or ⅛ pt wine
and ⅛ pt rum

2½ oz. castor sugar
3 large eggs
pinch cinnamon

Melt an ounce of butter and fry the breadcrumbs lightly. Add the wine or wine and rum and withdraw the pan from the heat. Transfer the contents to a bowl and whisk. Leave to cool a little. Beat the remainder of the butter with the sugar and blend with the egg yolks. Add to the wine and breadcrumbs and stir. Beat the whites until very stiff and fold them into the mixture. Transfer to a buttered soufflé-dish and cook for about 30 minutes (400°F, Mark 6) until well browned and risen. Serve with rum sauce (p. 111) or cream.

SWEET OMELET WITH FRUIT SAUCE

(serves 4)

SAUCE
½ lb. morello cherries or berries in
season
½ pt water
sugar to taste (about 2 oz.)
1 dessertspoon potato flour, cornflour
or arrowroot
1 egg-white

OMELET
3 eggs
1 tablespoon plain flour
1 heaped tablespoon sugar
rind of ½ lemon
butter for frying

The sauce should be half ready before you start the omelet.

CHERRY SAUCE: Stalk, wash and carefully stone the cherries. Boil them in the water with sugar for about ten minutes until tender. Lift them out of the water with a perforated spoon and keep them warm. When the omelet is nearly ready bring the liquid back to the boil and thicken it with the potato flour mixed with a little water. Stir and allow to simmer for a few minutes. Beat the egg-white till it is very stiff. Remove the liquid from the heat and fold in the egg-white.

BERRY SAUCE: Stalk and wash the fruit and cook it in water with the sugar for about 20 minutes until tender. Put through a sieve. When the omelet is almost ready thicken the sauce with a dessertspoon of potato flour mixed with a little water. Stir until the mixture thickens. Beat the white of the egg until stiff. Remove the liquid from the heat and fold in the egg-white. Serve with the omelet.

OMELET: Beat the yolks with the sugar and sifted flour until white. Add the grated lemon rind. Beat the whites until they stand in peaks and fold them into the mixture. Heat a large omelet pan, melt the butter and pour in the mixture. This will take longer to cook than an ordinary omelet. If it is to be served with cherry sauce put the whole cherries across it before folding over.

ZEPHYR

(serves 6)

1 pt double cream	½ lb. either strawberries, raspberries
3 oz. castor sugar	or 6 stoned plums
grated rind of 1 lemon	6 meringues (optional)

Beat the cream until it is thick. Stalk and wash the fruit. If you use large strawberries or dessert plums cut them in quarters. Mix the fruit, sugar and lemon rind with the cream. Put it into a suitable serving-dish and chill. Decorate with meringues if you wish and serve with sweet biscuits or sponge fingers.

SNOWBALLS

(serves 6)

1½ pts milk	6 eggs
1 vanilla pod or grated rind of 1 lemon	4–6 oz. sugar (according to taste)

Slit the vanilla pod and put it in a saucepan with the milk. Bring to the boil. Meanwhile, beat the egg-whites until they stand in peaks. Put tablespoons of the beaten egg-whites into the boiling milk to cook. When they rise to the surface they are ready. Lift out with a perforated spoon and put on a large plate to cool.

Beat the egg yolks with the sugar until white. Remove the vanilla pod, allow the milk to cool slightly and add. Mix well and cook over a low heat, stirring all the time until the mixture resembles a thick cream. On no account allow it to boil. Add the grated lemon rind at this stage if you are using it instead of the vanilla pod. Pour the custard into a shallow dish and float the snowballs on top. Chill and serve.

EGG CUSTARD

(serves 4)

4 egg yolks	1 pt milk
2 oz. sugar	1 vanilla pod

Beat the egg yolks with the sugar until white. Heat the milk in a saucepan with the slit vanilla pod. Bring to the boil and put aside to cool slightly. Pour the milk with the vanilla pod over the egg and sugar mixture. Stir and transfer the custard to the saucepan. Cook on a very low heat, stirring all the time, till the mixture resembles a thick cream. Do not let it boil. Remove the vanilla pod and serve hot or cold.

SABAYON

(serves 4)

5 egg yolks
2½ oz. vanilla sugar
grated rind of 1 lemon

2 wineglasses sherry (port or
madeira)

Beat the vanilla sugar with the egg yolks until white and fluffy. Add the sherry and lemon rind and cook over a low heat, stirring all the time, until it resembles a thick cream. Do not let it boil. Serve alone, hot or cold, or with fruit salad.

GOGOL MOGOL

Per person:
1 egg yolk
1 level tablespoon castor sugar

1 teaspoon rum or brandy (optional)
2 wafers

Beat the sugar with the egg yolk until white. Stir in a teaspoon of rum or brandy. Pour into an individual dish. Chill and serve with wafers.

LEMON WATER ICE

(serves 4)

¾ pt water
6 oz. sugar
slice of lemon rind

juice of 1 large lemon
handful redcurrants (optional)

Boil the sugar and water with a thin strip of lemon rind for a few minutes. Cool. Add the lemon juice. Strain the liquid into a container and freeze. Decorate with redcurrants before serving.

VANILLA ICE-CREAM

(serves 6)

6 *egg yolks*	1½ *pts milk or single cream*
6 *oz. sugar*	1 *vanilla pod or grated rind of* 1 *lemon*

Beat the egg yolks and sugar with a wooden spoon until white. Put the milk or cream in a saucepan with the slit vanilla pod and bring it to the boil. Remove from the heat and leave for a few minutes. Add the eggs and sugar and stir. Return to the saucepan and cook very slowly over a low heat for about 5–10 minutes, stirring all the time until the mixture resembles a thick cream. Don't let it boil. If lemon rind is used instead of a vanilla pod it should be added now. Cool. When the custard is quite cold transfer it to a bowl. Stand this bowl in a larger bowl containing as many ice cubes as possible. Add a little cooking salt to the ice and whip the custard with a whisk or rotary beater until it thickens. Transfer it to the ice tray in the fridge to use when required. Serve with wafers.

COFFEE ICE-CREAM

Follow the recipe for Vanilla ice-cream adding 3 teaspoons of strong coffee to the milk instead of the vanilla pod.

CHOCOLATE ICE-CREAM

Follow the recipe for vanilla ice-cream adding 3 heaped teaspoons of cocoa mixed with a little water to the milk instead of the vanilla pod.

STRAWBERRY ICE-CREAM

(serves 6)

4 egg yolks
½ lb. sugar
1 pt double cream

3 tablespoons rose water
1 lb. strawberries

Beat the egg yolks and sugar with a wooden spoon until white. Add the cream and transfer to a saucepan. Cook very slowly over a low heat, stirring all the time until the mixture resembles a thick cream. On no account allow it to boil. Add the rose water and cool.

Stalk and wash the fruit. Put it through a sieve. There should be about half a pint of purée. Add the sieved berries to the cream and blend well. Transfer the mixture to a bowl and stand the bowl in a larger bowl containing as many ice cubes as possible. Add a little cooking salt to the ice and whip the custard with a whisk or rotary beater until it thickens. Transfer to the ice tray in the fridge.

This can also be made with raspberries.

ORANGE RICE

(serves 4–6)

4 oz. rice
5 oz. sugar
2 large oranges or 4 small

2 cloves
⅔ pt water

Boil the rice in plenty of salted water until ready but not overdone. Take care not to overcook it as this will spoil the pudding. It should take about 20 minutes.

Transfer the rice to a colander when ready and run cold water through to get rid of the starch and to separate the grains. Drain completely and put into a bowl to cool.

While the rice is cooking, make a syrup by boiling $2\frac{1}{2}$ oz.
sugar with $\frac{1}{3}$ pt water for a few minutes. Allow to cool.
When cold pour over the rice.

Remove the rind from the oranges with a sharp knife and
using half the peel only cut up small as for marmalade.
Remove the pith and any pips from the oranges, and cut
into thin slices. Place the orange slices in a large serving-
dish.

Now boil the rest of the sugar and water briskly with the
orange peel and cloves for 5 minutes. Allow to cool.

When the rice is quite cold spread it over the oranges.
Pour over the cold syrup with the peel and allow to drain to
the bottom of the dish, making the orange slices moist. This
is a most refreshing pudding. It is also easy to prepare and
the ingredients are always handy.

RICE LAYER PUDDING

(serves 6)

1 pt milk	1 oz. sugar
2 oz. rice	6 oz. approx. jam or apple purée from
pinch of salt	1 lb. apples (see p. 111)
$\frac{1}{2}$ vanilla pod	butter for cooking
2 egg yolks	

Put the rice, milk, salt and half a vanilla pod in a saucepan
and bring to the boil. Simmer slowly for 15–20 minutes,
stirring frequently until it thickens. Cool slightly and remove
the vanilla pod.

Beat the egg yolks with the sugar until white and add to
the rice. Butter a fireproof dish and put in layers of rice
and layers of jam or apple purée, ending in a rice layer.
Brown in a moderate oven (325°F, Mark 3) for about 20
minutes. Serve hot or cold with egg custard (see p. 156).

RICE PUDDING WITH PUMPKIN

(serves 6)

1 lb. pumpkin	1 pt milk
1 oz. sugar	pinch salt
2 oz. rice	

Peel the piece of pumpkin and remove any seeds. Chop into cubes. Cook with the sugar in a little water for about 10–15 minutes. Put the rice, milk and salt in another saucepan and simmer slowly for 15–20 minutes, stirring frequently, until it thickens. When it is ready, add the cooked pumpkin which can be mashed if you wish. Put the mixture in a fireproof dish and bake for 20–30 minutes (325°F, Mark 3) in the oven. Serve with sugar. Millet can be substituted for rice in this recipe.

RICE WITH FRUIT SAUCE

(serves 4–5)

4 oz. rice	juice of ¼ lemon
1 oz. currants	2 tablespoons vanilla sugar
1 oz. sultanas	½ pt Berry Kissel (see p. 149)
rind of ½ lemon, grated	pinch of salt

Put the rice, currants, sultanas and salt in a muslin bag, leaving room for it to expand and boil for about 20 minutes. Meanwhile, squeeze the juice from the lemon and stir into it the grated rind and 1 tablespoon sugar. Mix thoroughly.

When the rice is ready, transfer to a colander, remove the muslin and pour cold water through to remove starch and separate the grains. Drain thoroughly. Mix with the sugar and lemon juice. Transfer to a suitable mould which has been rinsed in water and dusted with 1 tablespoon sugar.

Press down with a spoon to make the top even. Cool. When
cold turn out on to serving-dish and pour over the Kissel
which should be made as a sauce with half the quantity of
flour.

alternative sauce

½ lb. raspberries, strawberries or 2–3 oz. sugar
 redcurrants   ⅛ pt water
           ⅛ pt red or white wine

Stalk and wash the fruit and rub it through a sieve.
Put 2–3 oz. of sugar, depending on the type of fruit, in a
saucepan with the water and bring to the boil. Add the wine
and the sieved fruit. Bring to the boil again, stir and remove
any scum which has formed. Serve the sauce either hot or
cold with the hot rice.

CHOCOLATE AND VANILLA RICE PUDDING

(serves 6)

2 oz. rice   ½ vanilla pod
1 pt Jersey milk   2 egg yolks
2 oz. sugar   2 oz. grated chocolate

Put the rice, milk, half a vanilla pod and 1 tablespoon of
sugar into a saucepan and cook very slowly for about 20
minutes, stirring frequently. Cool and remove the vanilla
pod.

Beat the egg yolks with the remaining sugar and mix with
half the rice. Mix the grated chocolate with the other half.
Put layers of chocolate and vanilla rice into a buttered fireproof dish, ending with a vanilla layer. Brown in a moderate
oven (325°F, Mark 3) for about 20–30 minutes. Cool and

turn out on to a dish. This pudding can be decorated with whipped cream and glacé cherries. Serve with chilled egg custard (see p. 156).

KUTIA

(serves 6)

½ lb. poppy seeds
1 oz. sugar
2 oz. shelled walnuts (optional)

2 tablespoons honey
2 oz. sultanas
8 oz. rice

Pour boiling water over the poppy seeds and allow them to stand for two to three hours. Put the seeds through a mincer two or three times, adding the sugar the last time. Dry the walnuts for about 10 minutes in the oven. Mix the seeds and sugar with the honey, sultanas and chopped walnuts.

Boil the rice until cooked and strain. Mix all the ingredients together and leave to stand for about two hours before serving.

Kutia can also be made from wheat grain instead of rice, if this is available.

GUREVSKAYA KASHA (1) (Semolina Pudding with Nuts)

(serves 6)

¼ lb. shelled almonds or walnuts
1 pt Jersey milk
1 oz. semolina
few drops almond essence
1½ oz. vanilla sugar

1 large egg
1 tablespoon granulated sugar
4 oz. jam or 8 oz. fresh fruit
    (optional)

Grate half the nuts and chop the other half. Heat the milk

in a saucepan and add the semolina just before it boils. Bring to the boil and simmer for several minutes until it is cooked, stirring all the time. It should have a thin consistency. Remove from the heat and add the nuts and almond flavouring. Beat the egg yolk with the vanilla sugar until white and add to the semolina mixture. Beat the egg-white until very stiff and fold it in. Transfer to a buttered pie-dish and sprinkle with the granulated sugar. Put the dish under a hot grill to caramelize the sugar. When golden brown put in a fairly hot oven (400°F, Mark 6) for 15–20 minutes. It will rise slightly. Eat hot with fruit compôte or jam and cold with fruit compôte and cream.

An alternative method is to put a layer of fresh fruit or jam between two layers of semolina mixture in the pie-dish and cook in the same way. The fruit must, of course, be suitably prepared: peeled, sliced and stoned as necessary.

GUREVSKAYA KASHA (2) (Semolina Pudding with Nuts and Cream)

(serves 8–10)

½ pt double cream
¼ lb. shelled almonds or walnuts
1 pt single cream
1 oz. semolina
few drops almond essence

2 oz. vanilla sugar
1 tablespoon granulated sugar
4 oz. jam or 12 oz. fresh fruit
   (optional)

Grate half the nuts and chop the other half. Put the cream in a fairly shallow basin and place under the grill or in a fairly hot oven (400°F, Mark 6). Skim off the brown skins as they form and put them in a dish, until half the cream has been used up. Warm the single cream in a saucepan and add the semolina. Stir quickly to prevent any lumps forming and boil for a few minutes until cooked. It should have a thin consistency. If it has thickened too much add a little milk. Add all the nuts, almond essence and vanilla sugar. Put half the cream skins on the bottom of a buttered pie-dish. Cover with half the semolina. Put the rest of the skins on top and end with a semolina layer. Sprinkle with granulated sugar and put under a hot grill to caramelize the sugar. When golden brown put in a fairly hot oven (400°F, Mark 6) for about 15 minutes to heat through. Serve with fruit compôte or jam. or put a layer of either fresh fruit or jam between layers of cream and semolina, and cook in the same way. The fruit should be prepared, i.e. stoned if necessary.

OLADY

(serves 8)

1 oz. yeast	2 eggs
1 tablespoon sugar	1 teaspoon salt
1 pt milk	1 lb. cooking apples
1 lb. plain flour	butter for frying

Mix the yeast in a little warm water with the sugar. Add the warm milk and sifted flour. Cover and leave to rise in a warm place for about half an hour. Add the beaten eggs and salt. Beat the mixture with a wooden spoon until it is smooth. Allow it to rise a second time. The batter is now ready.

Peel and core the apples and cut them in slices. Cut the slices in half if they are large. Coat the slices in batter and fry them in hot butter in a thick frying-pan, turning them when they are brown on one side. Serve with sugar or jam.

Olady can also be made as small pancakes without the apple and eaten with jam.

TVOROZHNIKY

(serves 6)

1 lb. curd cheese	rind of 1 lemon
1½ oz. flour	1 egg
1 oz. vanilla sugar	flour for coating
1 tablespoon sultanas (optional)	butter or oil for frying
pinch of salt	

Sieve the cheese to remove any lumps. Add the flour, vanilla sugar, sultanas, salt, grated lemon rind and egg. Mix well. Turn on to a floured board. Taking a tablespoonful of the mixture at a time form into small rissole shapes. Coat in flour and fry in butter or oil until golden brown. Sprinkle with sugar and serve with jam or a thin berry kissel (p. 149).

ZAPEKANKA OF CREAM CHEESE

(serves 6)

1 lb. curd cheese	1 tablespoon sultanas
4 eggs	rind of lemon or orange
1½ oz. melted butter	2 oz. candied peel
¼ lb. sugar	1 tablespoon dry breadcrumbs
1 oz. fine semolina	

Sieve the cheese and add the beaten egg yolks, melted butter, sugar and semolina and mix well with a wooden spoon until smooth. Add the washed sultanas, grated lemon or orange rind and chopped peel. Beat the egg-whites until very stiff and fold them into the mixture. Butter a fireproof dish and dust it with breadcrumbs. Transfer the mixture and bake in a moderate oven (400°F, Mark 6) for half an hour or until brown. Serve hot or cold with sour cream.

CHEESE BABA

(serves 4)

¾ lb. curd cheese
2 oz. sugar
1 tablespoon sultanas
lemon rind (optional)

1 tablespoon cream
1 egg
vanilla flavouring

Sieve the cheese and add the sugar. Bought cheese will need more than home-made. Add the washed sultanas, grated lemon rind, cream, beaten egg, and vanilla flavouring. Mix well and put into a greased baking-dish. Sprinkle with sugar and dot with butter. Bake in a moderate oven (375–400°F, Mark 5–6) for half an hour or till brown. Serve hot or cold with cream or sour cream.

Paskha

The word 'paskha' means 'Easter' in Russian and paskha is traditionally eaten at Easter together with kulich (see p. 143) and coloured eggs to break the long Lenten fast.

The paskha is made in a special mould made from five pieces of wood slotted together. It is in the shape of a pyramid with the letters 'XX' and 'BB' which means 'Christ is risen and truly he has risen'. The mould often has a cross on it as well.

FRESH PASKHA

(serves 12–14)

1 lb. 6 oz. sugar
5 egg yolks
½ pt. milk
1 vanilla pod
½ lb. fresh butter

3½ lb. curd cheese
1 tablespoon currants (optional)
grated lemon rind (optional)
2 oz. finely chopped blanched almonds
¼ pt double cream

Beat the egg yolks with ½ lb. of sugar until white. Add the milk and the vanilla pod and cook in a double boiler until the mixture thickens. Add the butter in very small pieces and allow it to melt. Cool.

Sieve the cheese into a large bowl to remove any lumps. Add the cooled custard and the remainder of the sugar. The mixture should be very sweet as a lot of the sugar will drain away. Add the lemon rind, cleaned currants and almonds. Whip the cream and add. Mix well.

Although Russians have a special wooden shape for making paskha it can equally well be made in a large flower-pot or colander lined with a piece of wet muslin folded double. Fill the receptacle with the paskha and fold the muslin over at the top. Stand it over a dish to catch the liquid that drains away and put a plate with a small weight on top of the muslin. Leave overnight in a cool place to drain. Turn out on to a large dish the following day. Cover with a damp napkin and keep in the fridge. The paskha should keep for about a week if the napkin is renewed every day. Serve with a slice of kulich.

COOKED PASKHA

(serves 10)

2½ lb. curd cheese	1 tablespoon cleaned currants
1 pt sour cream	grated lemon rind
5 eggs	1 lb. sugar
¼–½ lb. butter	1 oz. finely chopped blanched almonds
1 vanilla pod	

Sieve the cheese into a large bowl to remove any lumps. Add the sour cream, beaten eggs and butter. You will need about ½ lb. butter if you are using bought cheese; ¼ lb. should be enough for home-made. Transfer the mixture to a large saucepan and cook over a low heat, stirring all the time.

Do not let it boil. When cooked, the mixture will steam. This may take a fairly long time but it is most important to cook it properly. When ready, stand the saucepan in a large bowl of ice. Add a slit vanilla pod and seeds and a little grated lemon rind. When the mixture is quite cold add the sugar, almonds and currants. The amount of sugar will depend on whether the cheese is home-made or bought. (Bought cheese needs more.)

Drain and serve in the same way as fresh paskha (see above).

RASPBERRY PASKHA

(serves 8)

2 lb. curd cheese	¼ lb. unsalted butter
½ lb. raspberry jam (jelly)	½ pt. sour cream
6 oz. sugar	a little raspberry flavouring (optional)
3 eggs	

Sieve the cheese into a bowl to remove any lumps. Add the raspberry jam and the sugar and mix well. A few drops of raspberry flavouring may be added if desired. Beat the butter and add with the eggs and sour cream. Mix very well. A little more sugar may be necessary. Drain and serve in the same way as fresh paskha.

A NOTE ON CURD CHEESE

Curd cheese can vary considerably in quality and flavour so it is important to understand how to treat the different types. Home made cheese is fresh and therefore mild in flavour and needs very little sugar. In England shop-bought curd cheese is often sour, particularly in warm weather. To counteract this use fresh cream instead of sour and add an extra egg in the paskha recipes. If necessary more sugar may be used: up to

$\frac{1}{2}$ lb. sugar to 1 lb. of cheese. If you have a little home made cheese you may mix this with the bought cheese to improve the flavour. Always keep cheese in the fridge if possible.

Drinks

VISHNYOVKA

3 lb. morello cherries
2½ lb. granulated sugar
½ bottle vodka

Wash, stalk and carefully stone the cherries. Put the cherries and sugar in stone jars in alternate layers, ending with a sugar layer. Cover with muslin, and leave for three weeks in a warm place to ferment. When it has stopped fermenting add the vodka, cork the jars firmly and leave for a month or longer. Strain the liquid into bottles and seal. Leave nine months if possible.

The cherries, when discarded, can be dipped in castor sugar and eaten with Russian tea.

KRUSHÒN

¼ lb. sugar
¼ pt boiling water
1 small tin pineapple
2 bottles medium dry white wine
¼ bottle rum

Dissolve ¼ lb. sugar in ¼ pt boiling water. Cut the pineapple into small pieces. Put all the ingredients into a large bowl. Ice before serving and serve immediately as it will not keep.

TZAR'S PUNCH

½ lb. sugar
juice of 6 lemons
1 small tin crushed pineapple
½ bottle rum
juice of 3 oranges
1 bottle champagne

Heat the sugar in a little water over a low heat to make a syrup. Add the strained lemon juice. A clear syrup will form. Sieve the pineapple into a large bowl and pour in the hot syrup. Add the rum and cool. Add the strained orange juice and champagne. Serve iced.

BALALAIKA COCKTAIL

1 part vodka
1 part orange juice (fresh or tinned)
1 part soda water

Mix well and chill. Serve with a thin slice of lemon or orange.

KVASS

1 lb. black bread
2½ qts boiling water
½ oz. yeast

¼ lb. sugar
sprig of mint
½ oz. sultanas

Cut the bread in cubes and dry in a very slow oven for 1–2 hours. Be careful not to let it burn. Put the rusks in a bowl and pour in the boiling water. Cover with a cloth and leave for 3–4 hours. Strain through muslin and add the yeast, sugar and mint. Cover with a cloth and leave for 5–6 hours. When the kvass starts to foam strain it through muslin again and put it in bottles. Add a few sultanas to each bottle. Soak the corks in boiling water to make them more flexible and cork the bottles very securely. Replace the corks if they pop. Leave the bottles lying down in a cool place. The kvass should be ready in 2–3 days.

Kvass is similar in taste to a weak English beer. It is served with meals and can also be used as a stock for okroshka, borshch and other soups.

HOW TO SERVE VODKA

Vodka should be served in very small glasses as it is drunk in one gulp, never sipped. It is always iced and served with food, either with zakuski (see chapter one) or with any course of the meal, apart from the sweet. It is excellent with blini (see p. 130). A few thin slices of lemon or orange peel added several hours before serving give the drink a very pleasant flavour.

Miscellaneous

SOUR MILK

Milk should only take about twenty-four hours to go sour. If it takes longer it will have a bitter taste and can then only be used for baking. Pour the required amount of milk into a bowl and leave in a place in the kitchen where there are plenty of germs. Milk will not ferment in a clinically clean kitchen. When it is ready the sour milk will be like junket. Eat with sugar and black bread or use for making curd cheese.

CURD CHEESE

4 pts of milk will make approximately 1 lb. of curd cheese.

Make the sour milk (see above) in two bowls as it is then easier to handle. Cut the solid sour milk in four with a knife. This helps it to cook more quickly. The cream which forms on top of the sour milk can be skimmed off and used separately but the cheese will taste much better if it is left. Put the sour milk in a fireproof dish in a slow oven (250–300°F, Mark 1–2) for about 1½ hours until the curds have separated from the whey. Cool. Hang in a muslin bag over a large bowl to dry off.

Sieve, if lumpy, and mix with a tablespoon of washed sultanas and serve with sugar and sour cream, or use for making Paskha (p. 168) or Vatrushka (p. 129).

YOGHURT

1 pt best quality milk   *1 tablespoon bought yoghurt*

Use only the best quality milk as this has more cream and gives the yoghurt a far better flavour. Boil the milk in a saucepan for a few minutes and then cool to a temperature just above blood heat. Put into a bowl with a tablespoon of bought yoghurt. Cover with a plate and wrap the bowl round with several layers of cloth so that it retains the heat. Leave in a warm place for about 12 hours. It will set when cool. It differs from bought yoghurt in that it has a layer of cream on top. Serve with sugar or jam.

SOUR CREAM

Sour cream is not, of course, cream which has gone off. Cream which has gone off has a bitter taste and can only be used for baking. There are two ways of making sour cream:

1. Add a little lemon juice to fresh cream and stir. It should thicken immediately, but if not leave it to stand for a short time.

2. Allow the cream to sour naturally. This is very difficult in England since the cream is pasteurized and the weather is rarely very hot. Cream will not go sour in a clinically clean kitchen. If the cream has not thickened in 24 hours add lemon juice; otherwise the cream will go off and taste bitter.

Sour cream will keep for several days in the fridge. A little single cream or top of the milk can be added to prevent it thickening too much.

RAGENKA

1 pt best quality milk   1 tablespoon sour cream

This is similar to yoghurt but richer. Bake a pint of Jersey milk in a slow oven (250–300°F, Mark 1–2) for about $1\frac{1}{2}$–2 hours. The longer it is cooked, the richer the ragenka. A

brown skin will form on top as in a milk pudding. Take out
of the oven and cool to just above blood heat. Put a tablespoon of sour cream under the skin and leave in a warm
place to set. Eat when cold. Serve with sugar, jam or black
bread.

SALTED CABBAGE

2½ lb. hard white cabbage	6 peppercorns
1 oz. common salt	

Wash and drain the cabbage and remove the stalk and
outer leaves. Cut the cabbage in quarters. Line the bottom of
an earthenware jar with some of the whole cabbage leaves.
Shred the rest of the cabbage finely and sprinkle with the
salt. Pack it tightly in the jar together with the peppercorns.
Cover with some whole leaves. Tie a muslin cloth over the
top of the jar and cover this with a small plate. The cabbage
will go bad unless it remains covered all the time. Store in a
fairly warm place. In a few days, when the cabbage starts to
ferment, a foam will appear on the surface. When this dis-
appears, after about a week, the cabbage is ready for use and
can be stored in a cool, dry place until required. The muslin
may need washing during fermentation. If so, rinse it well in
cold water and replace.

A variation on plain salted cabbage can be achieved by
adding slices of a peeled apple and carrot and a tablespoon of
cleaned cranberries. If these are included an extra teaspoon of
salt will be needed. Serve with meat or poultry.

PICKLED MUSHROOMS

1 lb. mushrooms	3 peppercorns
⅛ pt wine vinegar	1 bayleaf
¼ pt water	2 cloves
¾ tablespoon common salt	

Use only one variety of mushrooms. They should be freshly picked, if possible. Discard the stalks and any unsound parts. Wash, drain well and peel. Cut in quarters if they are large; otherwise leave whole. Put the wine vinegar and water in a saucepan. Add the mushrooms and bring to the boil. Remove any scum and add the salt, peppercorns, bayleaf and cloves and simmer for about 20 minutes, stirring all the time. When the mushrooms settle on the bottom of the saucepan remove it from the heat. Cool, transfer to jars and seal. Serve as zakuski with vodka (see p. 173).

SLIGHTLY SALTED CUCUMBERS

3 lb. cucumbers	1 clove garlic
oak, blackcurrant, cherry or vine leaves	2 heaped tablespoons common salt
4 sprigs dill	2 pts water
4 peppercorns	

Use firm ripe ridge cucumbers about 3 inches long. Line the bottom of an earthenware jar with the leaves. Wash the cucumbers and stand them upright in the jar. Add the dill, peppercorns and garlic. Bring the saline solution to the boil. Be careful not to exceed the quantity of salt stated as too much will ruin this recipe. Cool and pour over the cucumbers and cover with a few more leaves. To make sure that the cucumbers remain immersed in the liquid all the time and do not float up, tie a muslin cloth over the top of the jar and put a saucer or plate on top. The leaves are important in this recipe as they help to prevent the cucumbers from going soft.

The cucumbers will be ready to eat in about a week. Serve as zakuski with vodka (see p. 173).

SALTED TOMATOES

3 lb. tomatoes
oak, blackcurrant, cherry or vine leaves
4 sprigs dill
1 2 peppercorns

1 clove garlic
2 heaped tablespoons common salt
2 pts water

Choose tomatoes of the same size, either small green ones or larger ripe ones. Use the same method as for salted cucumbers, packing them tightly in an earthenware jar. Note, however, that more peppercorns are used. They should be ready to eat in about a week. Serve as zakuski with vodka (see p. 173).

PICKLED GRAPES OR PLUMS

1 lb. grapes or plums
¼ pt wine vinegar
½ pt water
½ teaspoon salt

4 oz. sugar
2 peppercorns
1 clove

Remove the stalks and wash the grapes or plums. Put them into earthenware or bottling jars. Put the wine vinegar, water, salt, sugar, peppercorns and clove into a saucepan and bring to the boil. Cool and pour over the fruit. Cover the jars with greaseproof paper tied with string. They should keep for about 6 months in a cool place. Serve as zakuski with vodka (see p. 173) or with roast meat or poultry.

DILL

Dill is a herb which is widely used in Russia for salads and soups and as garnish for other dishes. It can be grown in the garden in the summer and dried at home for use in the winter. To dry, remove the stalks and leave the dill on clean sheets of paper for about two weeks, turning from time to time. When completely dry, rub gently between the hands and put into sealed jars. (Parsley can be dried and stored in the same way.) Dried dill is also obtainable in delicatessen shops.

VANILLA PODS AND VANILLA SUGAR

Vanilla can be used in two ways:

1. Cut the pod in half with a sharp knife and remove the seeds. If you are using milk in the recipe, put both the pod and the seeds in the milk and boil for a few minutes.

2. If you wish to keep the vanilla for future use, cut the pod in half with a knife and remove the seeds. Mix the pod and the seeds with castor sugar: 1 lb. sugar to each pod. Put into an airtight jar and keep in a cool, dry place. The vanilla sugar will be ready for use in about a week. It can be kept for a long time if stored in this way.

Oven Temperatures

	DEGREES FAHRENHEIT	GAS REGULO
Very slow	200 – 300	$\frac{1}{4}$ – 1
Slow	300 – 350	2 – 3
Moderate	350 – 375	4
Moderately hot	375 – 425	5 – 6
Hot	425 – 450	7
Very hot	450 – 500	8 – 9

Equivalent Weights and Measures

Fluid measures

One standard English cup holds 10 fluid ounces or half an English pint. One American cup on the other hand, holds 8 fluid ounces. One American cup is therefore equivalent to $\frac{2}{5}$ of an English pint.

Dry measures

These vary according to the density of the ingredient but the following table will serve as a basic guide.

ENGLISH	AMERICAN
1 lb. flour	4 cups sifted flour
½ lb. white sugar	1 cup
½ lb. brown sugar	1¼ cups
½ lb. fat	1 cup

METRIC	
1 oz.	approx. 28 gms.
1 lb.	approx. 450 gms.
1 pint	approx. ½ litre

Index

NOTES

NOTES

NOTES

NOTES

NOTES

NOTES

NOTES